D0104557

VIRGINIA WOOLF

A BEGINNER'S GUIDE

GINA WISKER

Series Editors
Rob Abbott & Charlie Bell
Drawings
Steve Coots

Hodder & Stoughton

A MEMBER OF THE HODDER HEADLINE GROUP

Orders: please contact Bookpoint Ltd, 39 Milton Park, Abingdon, Oxon OX14 4TD. Telephone: (44) 01235 400414, Fax: (44) 01235 400454. Lines are open from 9.00–6.00, Monday to Saturday, with a 24-hour message answering service. Email address: orders@bookpoint.co.uk

British Library Cataloguing in Publication Data
A catalogue record for this title is available from The British Library

ISBN 0 340 789093

First published 2000
Impression number   10 9 8 7 6 5 4 3 2 1
Year   2005 2004 2003 2002 2001

Drawings by Steve Coots
Typeset by Transet Limited, Coventry, England.
Printed in Great Britain for Hodder & Stoughton Educational, a division of Hodder Headline Plc, 338 Euston Road, London NW1 3BH by Cox & Wyman, Reading, Berks

CONTENTS

Introduction

HOW TO USE THIS BOOK

The *Beginner's Guide* series aims to introduce readers to the major writers of the past five hundred years. It is assumed that readers will begin with little or no knowledge and will want to go on to explore the named writer(s) in other ways. This book should be seen as a companion guide to the writer's major works: it is not a substitute for reading the works themselves. You will obtain a much fuller appreciation by reading as much of the author's work as possible and by consulting critical studies.

This book is divided into eight chapters. After considering how to approach the author's work and a brief biography, the book explores some of the author's main writings and themes before examining some critical approaches to the author. Finally there are suggestions for further reading and possible areas of further study.

HOW TO APPROACH UNFAMILIAR OR DIFFICULT TEXTS

Much writing in English is multi-layered and complex. It may contain incredibly long sentences; seemingly impenetrable prose; difficult shifts of time, space and viewpoint; or challenging ideas and concepts. Often writers go against convention and twist language for their own purposes. The effect of all this can be to make us confused, confounded, annoyed, amused, amazed, astonished or even put us off reading the text completely! The trick is to persevere. It is precisely this diversity and complexity which makes literature so rewarding and exhilarating.

There are several different modes of reading: for pleasure and entertainment; for insight into human life; for intellectual stimulation; for exploration of themes; for affirmation of what we think and hold dear; or for a challenge to our preconceptions. All of these are valid and are usually present simultaneously in literature.

Literature often needs to be read more than once, and in different ways. These ways can include: a leisurely and superficial reading to get the main ideas and narrative; a slower more detailed reading focusing on the nuances of the text, concentrating on what appear to be key passages; and reading in a random way, moving back and forth through the text to examine such things as themes, narrative or characterisation. Each reader has their own approach, but undoubtedly the best way to extract the most from a text is to read it several times.

In complex texts it may be necessary to read in short sections. Sometimes the only way to get by is to skip through the text, going back over it later. When it comes to tackling difficult words or concepts it is often enough to guess in context on the first reading, making a more detailed study using a dictionary or book of critical concepts on later reading. If you prefer to look up unusual words as you go along, be careful that you do not disrupt the flow of the text and your concentration.

Vocabulary

You will see that key terms and unfamiliar words are set in **bold** text. These words are defined and explained in the GLOSSARY to be found at the back of the book. In order to help you further we have also summarised each section in our SUMMARY sections.

You can read this introductory guide in its entirety, or dip in wherever suits you. You can read it in any order. It is a tool to help you appreciate a key figure in literature. We hope you enjoy reading it and find it useful.

✳ ✳ ✳ ✳ *SUMMARY* ✳ ✳ ✳ ✳

To maximise the use of this book:

- Read the author's work.

- Read it several times in different ways.

- Be open to innovative or unusual forms of writing.

- Persevere.

- Treat biographical information with care and concentrate mainly on the texts themselves.

ROB ABBOTT AND CHARLIE BELL – SERIES EDITORS

Why Read Virginia Woolf's Work Today?

1

Virginia Woolf's writing is as fresh today as at the beginning of the last century when it was written. Her insight into our emotions, feelings and thought processes shows a complex understanding of human nature that therapists would envy. She brings the changes in everyday relationships to life, evoking inner perceptions and presenting dialogues with a subtlety that is missing from TV serials and soaps. Her writing is sensitive and filled with the vitality of people's changing emotions.

A RADICAL WRITER

Her ability to challenge the traditional conventions of the novel is radical even by today's standards. She follows events and recreates them, representing life, rather than being enslaved by plot. Her perception about women's lives and about differences of experience based on gender, class or economics, is still very current. It enhances our understanding and articulation of problems and inequalities arising from a range of differences including geography, race, class, gender and economics, and heightens our awareness of the importance of recognising cultural difference and expression. Once you become involved in reading a novel by Virginia Woolf, you will love the delicacy and precision of her language and her lively, often wickedly perceptive, insight into our thoughts and behaviour.

AN EXPERIMENTAL WRITER

As a literary 'modernist' and experimental writer from the beginning of the twentieth century, Virginia Woolf's work has been considered far too difficult to read for pleasure. As a woman writer, her work has been said to concentrate on 'trivial' experiences, that is to say, the tensions and relationships of everyday experiences and everyday life. As a member of the rather intellectually elite **Bloomsbury group**, her work has been considered to concentrate only on the lives of the upper classes which are perceived as being rather distant to most readers. It is argued that she tends to focus on experiences and places only the wealthy would recognise – parties to which the prime minister is invited (*Mrs Dalloway*), large country houses in Cornwall (*To the Lighthouse*), and so on. Woolf's style, often labelled **stream of consciousness**, has also been found difficult to read.

Instead of writing about thoughts and descriptions of people and places in rather straightforward ways, Woolf plunges the

KEY TERMS

Bloomsbury group a group of philosophers, artists and writers whose intellect, wit and articulateness enabled them to set the pace in thinking, art and writing. They lived and worked in Bloomsbury in central London.

Stream of consciousness a new way of representing reality and experience as we feel it; the thoughts, feelings and sensations of an individual, all flowing together.

Woolf experiments with writing.

reader into the middle of a character's life and leaves the reader to try to discover who the characters are and what is happening. You have to read actively, to investigate and make deductions, as you do in real life. Of course, it is this kind of active readership which makes her writing so interesting and exciting.

Her lively concentration on life as it is experienced appeals to a very wide range of readers from 16-year-olds to academics, from adults who read for pleasure to those who seek a reading challenge which questions the traditional formulae of novels. Her writing is not merely for intellectuals. If you enjoy the irony and vitality of Jane Austen or a good TV drama, you will enjoy Woolf's unique way of capturing life and its contradictions.

LIFE FROM THE INSIDE

Woolf's novels are not dominated by plot, but manage to describe experiences from the inside, through thoughts and senses. She shows us how to express and record the kinds of mixed feelings and responses to those feelings we have, for example, sitting down to eat with a group of family and friends whom we both love and dislike (*To the Lighthouse*). Woolf has the ability to provoke us as the reader to consider how we respond in relation to our own feelings, as well as noting how other people around us respond and feel. For example, we read of reacting to the irritating and the loveable habits of partners, friends and relatives in *To the Lighthouse* or *The Waves*: looking back at thoughts, experiences and feelings from the past while experiencing the present, and also looking forward and speculating about the future. Woolf both questions what we mean by 'reality', which represents something different for each of us, and then captures the reality, experiences and feelings of her characters. She makes us much more aware both of *how* we actually experience and how we reflect on that experience. She makes us aware of how the experience can be explored and expressed in new forms, in what has been called experimental writing. This writing shifts in and out of consciousnesses, out of people's own words and images, thought patterns and particular ways of behaving, in and out of subjective thoughts and actual events.

Women readers often love Woolf's work because it makes such clear statements about life that many women can identify with. This is missing from other writers of Woolf's time – Wells, Bennett and Galsworthy – and only present in the most insightful moments in the work of other great **modernists** such as Lawrence and Joyce (who often tend to represent women from a male point of view). Her statements and the ways in which she writes of women's consciousness, values, experiences and beliefs have revolutionised the way women have written since. Her work has emphasised different priorities in women's and men's lives. It has focused on the importance of exploring and expressing inner feelings, not just outward actions. It has argued that women might not only value different experiences from men, but might want to express and describe them using different kinds of language, expression and images.

> **KEY TERM**
>
> Modernism is a term used to describe the literary movement of the 1890s–1940s whose international writers numbered among them T.S. Eliot, Virginia Woolf, James Joyce and Ezra Pound. They wanted to write in a new way, rejecting the tired conventions of the nineteenth century and wished to 'make it new'. Complex technically, they often concentrated on disillusionment, fragmentation, and a search for something to believe in.

This insight into different values, experiences and expressions between the two genders has also, latterly, opened up our thoughts about how people from different backgrounds in terms of race, age, class, geography, education and so on, might want to write and read about experiences in different ways. It has enabled us as readers to understand that these ways are as legitimate, interesting and valuable as the more traditional, often rather middle-class, white male-oriented forms which have prevailed in literature.

Woolf's work and ideas have informed many of the great feminist thinkers, novelists and poets. Her radical and experimental writing laid a foundation for them, but Woolf's own statements about difference are not restrictively feminist; in fact, she argued that if we concentrate on gender differences alone they will skew what we write about and how we write it.

Her work appeals equally to male readers, particularly those who want to explore how we think and relate to one other and how we make sense of big questions in life such as its meaning, the effects of the passage of time, and what has lasting qualities. Such thoughts and questions she asks directly, through her characters. For example, Mr Ramsay (*To the Lighthouse*) wonders what lasts of all our achievements; Mrs Ramsay asks how men and women continue to love and live together. Bernard (*The Waves*) points out that we are all made up of the experiences and friends we have.

Woolf has also produced some very informative, lucid criticism and analysis of other writers.

✳ ✳ ✳ ✳*SUMMARY* ✳ ✳ ✳ ✳

- Woolf challenges the conventions of the novel.

- She brings a freshness of representation and expression of experience into language.

- She shows insight into thoughts, feelings, senses, memories, hopes and fears.

- Her writing has insights into relationships and their changing flow.

- Her work challenges representations and treatment of women.

- It challenges the limitations of strict, reductive logic.

- She has developed different kinds of writing – forms and images and sentence structures to express lived experience.

2 How to Approach Woolf's Work

Virginia Woolf is a fascinating experimental writer. She engages with an insider view of people's thoughts and feelings. She is also sharply aware of pomposity, hypocrisy and silliness, and sensitive to the slightest changes in moods and relationships between people. It sounds quite surprising then that many have found her work hard to read. It is certainly worth persevering with, because the rewards are so great. Once you are familiar with her tone and insights, the way she organises her sentences to fit thought movements rather than fixed formal patterns, you will wonder why you ever found her work hard going.

Virginia Woolf's reputation for being difficult arises largely from her refusal to humour the reader by providing pen portraits of each character or historic, realistic details of the context, background and setting. Instead she tends to plunge us into the middle of her tales and, often into the latter part of a sentence or an experience. In this she is likened to her modernist contemporaries – Joyce, Forster and Mansfield – who wanted to capture reality and 'lived experience' rather than conform to what we expect of a novel.

To the Lighthouse is a good example of her methods at their best. In order to appreciate Virginia Woolf, active reading is needed. The reader needs to piece together the information and reflections provided putting together the story and characters, interpreting themes and arguments. Woolf is an expert at recording experiences, sensations, thoughts and feelings of an individual in specific moments, and also of a number of people, relating to each other, over time. This latter is called **intersubjectivity**.

KEYWORD

Intersubjectivity How different people's responses affect each other. Woolf concentrates on a group of friends or family and shows how their feelings about each other affect their attitudes and actions, and are also influenced by thoughts of the past and the future.

Although Woolf looks in detail at inner feelings and responses, she comments on how these are sparked off by and relate to the external world, to social change, historical and political moments. Her novels are set in the period between the two world wars. One key theme is the way in which social relationships between men and women are experienced.

TO THE LIGHTHOUSE

Have a look at the opening page of *To the Lighthouse*. This is a significant passage because it exemplifies Woolf's style of stream of consciousness and intersubjectivity. *To the Lighthouse* emphasises new ways of writing about feelings. It is unconventional, because it refuses to sketch in all the details a realistic text would sketch in, such as time, place, character, and setting.

Stream of consciousness

The stream of consciousness form was first formally used by a French novelist called Edward Dujardin, whose novel *Les Lauriers Sont Coupeés* was itself influenced by a French philosopher and writer, Henri Bergson. In England, a novelist called Dorothy Richardson also began to write in stream of consciousness in her early 1921 work, *Pilgrimage*. Stream of consciousness was not just a literary innovation. It actually derived – as did so much innovation in modernist writing – from new ways of considering how we experience the world. William James, Henry James's brother (the author of *Turn of the Screw* and *Portrait of A Lady*) felt that experience was not made up of discreet elements but rather flowed together, each element of it affecting the other. In expressing experience in literature, Woolf felt we needed to capture this flow. What results is writing which captures what philosophers call 'sense impression' – our sense of smell, sound, touch, hearing – i.e. what we experience. It also captures thought patterns that often appear in symbols, rhythms or images and yet have to be translated into words to make any sense to the thinker (as if in fiction to the reader). To express this *felt* lived reality and *felt* sense of time

Woolf developed stream of consciousness. In this form, sense impressions, the flow of time, the influence of the past, future and present together, the changing ways in which people view and try to find the words to express their feelings are all represented in words.

Family interaction

If we look at the opening two pages of the first part of *To the Lighthouse* we find Woolf's style in full flow. The first page opens with an answer to a question relating to whether they will be able to visit the lighthouse – and we have to assume what the question is. Mrs Ramsay tells her son that if it is fine weather they can go to the lighthouse, which is the journey he is most set on, while they are staying in the holiday home on the coast. This gives us a sense of family interaction typical of the changes taking place between parents and children who both have very set designs and hopes. James's mother, Mrs Ramsay, does not want to disappoint him. Her sense of possibility transfers to James. James now feels 'an extraordinary joy'. The expedition seems settled, he can look forward to it. Woolf moves out from James's perspective and comments on how many of us feel that our hopes and fears for the future affect the experiences of the present. She comments that such people (including us) find the moment affected by the kinds of feelings they have. This is very perceptive – think back to important moments that have been made or marred by other activities and atmospheres at the same time. Woolf tells us something about our inner experiences and feelings, the importance we attach to events and activities, rather than merely detailing these events and activities as if divorced from the responses they generate.

There is also irony here, a sensitive amusement at a mother's responses to her son and a son's to his mother and father. James, a child, is sitting and cutting out a picture from the Army and Navy store catalogue. He then transfers his feelings about the potential lighthouse visit, to the cutting out task. The refrigerator, we are told, is 'fringed with joy'. This is funny – the refrigerator has nothing to do with the trip, but the activity James is involved in is affected by his feelings about the future. And so we see Woolf showing us that the past and the future have a great effect upon the present, how the differently timed moments turn into and affect each other, how feelings affect actions, sensations overlap. James is happy for a moment when he feels his wish is to be fulfilled, but part of the happiness is due to being with his mother whose nature is naturally to concede, to try to ensure that the family are happy, get their own way and work together. As he radiates happiness and transfers this happiness to the things he cuts out, she thinks of him very differently from the way he thinks of himself. She sees him as rather severe, and looks forward to his future job, maybe 'stark and uncompromising' as a judge. This is a typical mother thinking about her son. Mrs Ramsay wants James to be happy and successful and so offers the thought that the trip could well be on. Not so Mr Ramsay, who then enters with his version and answer. James's father, not a social being or a family type, needs to assert his own logic and order on what he sees as messy and unlikely. He does not want any one of his children to go along with something that feels unrealistic. So he denies the possibility of the trip; he casts a cold wet blanket over the activity and he says no.

James's response to his father's refusal is immediate, imaginative, and violent, 'Had there been an axe handy, or a poker, or any weapon that would have gashed a hole in his father's head and killed him there and then, James would have seized it. Such were the extremes of emotion that Mr Ramsay excited in his children's breasts by his mere presence'. This has been seen as an Oedipal response (named after the Oedipus complex which was a term arising from the Greek legend about Oedipus who killed his father and married his mother). James clearly prefers his mother and hates his father or rather, hates the controls and denials of his father. The response can only be translated at that age to violence but it plumbs the surprising depths of the child's feelings, and their immediacy. One minute he felt fine, the next, after the comment, he wants to attack his father.

Woolf shows us how the words and actions of one person cause huge changes in behaviour in another. She has stated all this, but has translated James's mind, a mind which contains more pictures than words and is filled with emotions. The next passage moves on in James's thought processes, seeing Mr Ramsay as 'lean as a knife' standing sarcastically, grinning, his main intent to disillusion James. As Mr Ramsay is being described according to James, the narrative voice slips into Mr Ramsay's own version of himself, into his mind. It does not record all his feelings, but starts to use the kind of phrases he would use to represent his feelings and thoughts. This is called **free indirect speech**.

Mr Ramsay appears totally uncompromising, and proud of never tampering with a single fact. His language becomes assertive, opinionated, philosophical and slightly biblical, talking of his children as being sprung from his 'loins'. The narrative voice captures his thoughts, then tells us, in brackets, what he actually *does*. This is most unusual. Most writers tell us what people do, and then

KEY TERM

Free indirect speech Captures someone's words without actually quoting what they say – it projects us into their mind.

KEY FACT

Jane Austen is credited with first using free indirect speech. This form of expression is a way of accessing the way someone thinks and expresses themselves. It works by describing the scene using the kinds of phrases and images that a person would use. So the flow is not jerking from character's thoughts to character's thoughts but smooth. It is an adopting of the kinds of language and expressions the character would use – to describe what they are doing or represent their feelings. It slips from one to the other and forms a shared experience.

imagine or record what they think, giving priority to actions rather than dwelling on thoughts. Woolf feels that the way we experience reality is mediated through our emotions and thoughts, so these take priority in her writing over actions.

Woolf moves from mind to mind, showing how each person affects the other. But she does not leave us flailing around wondering what to think. She sums up, directs our reading and interpretation. She tells us

Woolf's consciousness not confined.

early on that James, like so many others of us, mixes his feelings together and lets the past and future influence the present. Woolf here effectively tells us how her style operates, he 'cannot keep this feeling separate from that, but must let future prospects, with their joys and sorrows, cloud what is actually at hand'.

Symbols

Note Woolf's use of symbols. Mrs Ramsay is knitting a sock for the lighthouse keeper's son, and in this she is itemising different strands of wool as she itemises different feelings, handles the emotions of different family members, shows that she is able to respond to diversity, is flexible and varied herself, as well as maternal. Mr Ramsay is compared to sharp instruments, knives, like the axe and poker with which his son wants to hit him. This is in opposition to the interweaving, creative warm symbols of Mrs Ramsay. People in Woolf's novels are often recognisable by the symbols that attach to them. This is true also of *Mrs Dalloway*. Peter Walsh walks around fingering his pocket knife rather threateningly, his invasiveness and sexual interests are shown to us by his symbolic behaviour. Actions do not speak louder than words in Woolf – inner thoughts and feelings are more properly the object of her work.

Thoughts

Look at how Woolf moves between different people's thoughts in the passage in *To the Lighthouse* where she sits them all down to dinner, and Mrs Ramsay hands William Bankes a particularly nice piece of food because she suddenly feels sorry for him, alone and unmarried. People's thoughts and feelings flow and change according to mood and others' actions. What they say and do is less mentioned here than what is going on in their minds as they think about doing something, about their own feelings, or about other people. We are inside a mind rather than outside with actions.

Those reading Virginia Woolf for the first time will be interested in the way she captures experiences, perceptions and relationships. Look at how very well she records the variations in people's feelings, their ways of looking at the world. Woolf does not want the emphasis to be on times and fixed events and characters, but it often helps us as readers to construct a version of the story, time and characterisation from the novels in order to put the interactions into context.

When reading her essays the arguments are more straightforward but they are always illustrated by little vignettes or stories about people, e.g. Shakespeare's sister Judith (a fictional character) or Mary Carmichael (both in 'A Room of One's Own'), a woman who can study and write because of family economic support. Something not to miss is Woolf's irony – she is very observant and often quite ironic, not as serious as some would argue.

∗ ∗ ∗ ∗ SUMMARY ∗ ∗ ∗ ∗

- Woolf uses stream of consciousness as a new way of representing reality.

- She concentrates on thoughts rather than actions.

- Symbols are important in her work.

Biography and Influences

3

There is a whole branch of critical attention devoted to linking Woolf's life and her art. Some feminist critics argue that women such as Woolf deliberately engage their art with their lives, writing fiction with autobiographical elements. Others, however argue that her work should not be read in relation to the autobiographical details.

Two very good works on Woolf's life are *Virginia Woolf and her World* by John Lehman, which is filled with photographs and excerpts from original manuscripts, and the more recent *Virginia Woolf* by Hermione Lee (1996).

EARLY LIFE

Virginia Woolf's parents were artistic and intellectual. Her mother Julia Duckworth, nee Jackson, was one of the seven Pattle sisters who were well known for their artistic contributions in London. Leslie Stephen, Virginia's father, was a distinguished man of letters and the first editor of the *Dictionary of National Biography*. Virginia (born 1882) had one sister, Vanessa, and two brothers, Thoby and Adrian. Also in the household were Julia's children from her first marriage, notably Stella Duckworth, who was very close to Virginia. They lived at 22 Hyde Park Gate. Virginia gained the free run of her father's library, initially directed then left to read what she wished. She was taught at home by her governess, Janet Case, who became a close friend. Their holiday home in St Ives became the setting for *To the Lighthouse* (which features the Godrevy lighthouse off St Ives). It is mostly an autobiographical novel, recalling Virginia's parents and the liveliness of interaction among the children. Thoby and Virginia started a little weekly handwritten magazine between them as had the Bröntes before them. It was called *Hyde Park Gate News* and here her first writing appeared.

Sadly, their mother, Julia, died in 1895 when Virginia was only 13, and Stella took over running the household. Virginia, traumatised by her loss, had her first breakdown. In later life she had a number of other breakdowns, and suffered from depression. When Stella married Jack Hills, another loss took place. Only two years after Julia had died, Stella, returning ill from honeymoon, also died. Leslie Stephen, was gloomy, self pitying and dominant. During this very difficult period, Virginia was molested, first by George Duckworth then later Gerald, both her half brothers. They capitalised upon their family closeness and Virginia's vulnerability. They damaged her emotionally as a consequence. After the death of Sir Leslie Stephen, the family moved to 46 Gordon Square, which was part of what gradually became Bloomsbury, today a literary centre to the University of London. Thoby brought his Cambridge university friends here and involved his sisters Virginia and Vanessa in intellectual discussions.

DEATH OF THOBY

Virginia's next great sadness was the death of Thoby. Virginia, Vanessa, Thoby and a friend, Violet Dickinson had all travelled to Greece on holiday. Thoby, Vanessa and Violet all caught typhoid from drinking unboiled milk and Thoby died upon their return. Virginia never recovered from his death and in *The Waves* immortalised him as Percival, a central figure. Only two days after Thoby's death, Vanessa married Clive Bell. Virginia and her younger brother, Adrian, moved to 29 Fitzroy Square.

THE BLOOMSBURY GROUP

Bloomsbury group – a blast of fresh air.

What followed was an exciting and intellectually stimulating period in which Virginia, Adrian and friends presided over an intellectual grouping composed of writers, philosophers and artists which met regularly. The Bloomsbury group, as they were called, influenced each other's work, criticised each other's work, and commented on the work of other writers of the period. Artists Roger Fry and Duncan Bell were part of this group as was the novelist E.M. Forster. While Woolf influenced and was influenced by the thinkers, writers and artists around her, she was also interested in the writing of Katherine Mansfield, which she admired. Woolf and her husband, Leonard Woolf, would invite great writers such as T.S. Eliot to stay in the country and numerous photographs exist of her with great writers and thinkers, such as Lytton Strachey.

WOOLF'S SENSE OF HUMOUR

Virginia Woolf is often thought of as being intensely serious, but the 1910 Dreadnought hoax most surely put paid to this. Virginia and a friend dressed up as the Emperor of Abyssynia and entourage and paid a state visit to the newly commissioned HMS Dreadnought, to be well received, their hoax unquestioned. Their escapade even appeared in the *Daily Mirror* as a record of an official visit. Virginia Woolf's part in the hoax caused a family furore, but is evidence of her sense of humour and subversive mind.

Woolf began her work with the women's campaign at the run up to the First World War. Violence against women was experienced throughout the period of the struggle for the votes for women franchise and some elements of this are explored in *The Years* and in 'Three Guineas'.

ILLNESS AND PRODUCTIVITY

The Woolfs ran the Hogarth Press which published the work of many young writers, and employed friends and family in its running. Virginia and Leonard Woolf made an intellectually daunting couple who each needed a great deal of freedom. Leonard's Jewishness was a cause of conversation during the first year of her marriage, as this made him an unusual match at that time. In 1915 she suffered several breakdowns and Leonard began to control her, in her words 'turning her into an invalid'. Some of her reactions and painful expressions, portrayed in letters and diaries, are related to her sense of childlessness, some to his control, some to her potential for breakdown and what has been termed madness. During the early years of marriage photographs show Virginia surrounded by friends and by family as Vanessa's children grew up. Her diaries and letters from this time talk of her lonely creative task as a writer, which sometimes seems to be in opposition to her need for friends and family. She speaks of being 'wedged in her work with interruptions and at best potent and alive, washed by the food...of my own thoughts' and her 'various and gregarious' identity with others. *Mrs Dalloway*, a very innovative novel, was written from 1922–24, and was powerfully filled with the life of London, the joys as well as the doubts and pains of the post-war era.

Beginning to write *To the Lighthouse* at Monks House in 1925, Woolf comes close to psychoanalysis in exploring and expressing elements of her parents' lives and her childhood through the novel. It evokes the imperialism of the Ramsays, the word feminist is never used in the novel though Lily is clearly one, and Mr Ramsay emerges as a heroic tyrant, while Mrs Ramsay is seen as a charismatic earth mother and matriarch. In her book about Virginia Woolf, Hermione Lee calls it a book of loss and grief and yet, as she points out, it starts and finishes with ten-word sentences, both starting with the word 'Yes', which is seen by many as a sign of affirmation.

Around this time, Virginia Woolf met and gradually fell in love with Vita Sackville-West. Vita and her husband, Harold Nicholson, both wrote and broadcast on alternative ideas about marriage. 'In all London, you and I alone like being married', wrote Virginia to Vita in 1925, partly joking, partly ironic. Their relationship led to some trips away and the portrayal of Vita as Orlando in Virginia's novel.

DEEP DEPRESSION

In *The Waves*, written 1929–31, Woolf's experimentation reaches a new high. Coinciding with her involvement with activism, she wrote a diary commenting on defining self and reality, self and the outer world, themes which are explored in the novel. She read papers to the London society for women's service and her pacifist feminist material began appearing, which inspired both 'Three Guineas' and *The Years*. Woolf was a pacifist, and when World War II broke out, she recorded the deprivations their lives faced. She had often been depressed when finishing a novel and completing *The Years*, coupled with fears about the war, were too much for her.

Melancholia was always present.

A cold winter, disillusion at her writing and living in the country all contributed to her depression. One cold morning Virginia Woolf filled her pockets with stones drowned herself in the River Ouse.

✳✳✳✳**SUMMARY**✳✳✳✳

- Woolf was born in 1882.

- Woolf was abused by her two half brothers.

- She was very affected by the death of her older brother, Thoby.

- She founded Hogarth Press 1917 with her husband, Leonard.

- She was a member of the influential Bloomsbury group.

- Virginia suffered mental illness throughout her life.

- She had a lesbian affair with Vita Sackville-West.

- She drowned herself in the River Ouse in 1941.

Virginia Woolf – Major Themes

> Woolf is the only twentieth century British woman writer who is taken
> seriously by critics of all casts (Bowlby 1988)

Yet Woolf has quite a contradictory reputation and reception, often
because critics and readers want to categorise her as a certain kind of
writer, but she defies some of the simplistic rules they try to apply to
her. She writes of women and women's lives and generates discussion
about a woman's creative form of expression, but she was not an ardent
feminist, nor an active suffragette. She is a modernist in terms of her
writing experiments, choosing to represent reality and experience
using new techniques of writing. She broke with conventional
expression and constructions (seen as male or 'patriarchal') and wrote
about women's everyday lives, but yet was also seen as too concerned
with Bloomsbury aesthetics.

WOOLF AS A WOMAN/WRITER ON WOMEN AND WRITING

The impressive reputation and influence of Woolf as a great writer has
had a profound effect on the critical appreciation of women's writing
during the twentieth century. Her work is so innovative and well
written that she is taken seriously by a whole variety of critics. This
opened the door for further serious attention of the work of other
women writers of her own time, as well as drawing attention to the
works of women writers of earlier periods. Woolf's work focuses on the
issues and practices of what it means to be a woman writer, the topics,
the language and the ways in which women see and write about the
world. Woolf argued that women's experiences are different from those
of men, so it is not surprising that they would want to write and read
about such experiences rather than those which interest men. The
conventional topics of novels and poetry are not, she argues, the only
ones nor the normal or right ones, just those that happened to have
been established by certain kinds of male writers (e.g. Arnold Bennett

and H.G. Wells). She argues that men are interested in sport, wars and power, while women are more interested in the social experience and personal interaction. Not surprisingly then, women also want to express their experiences and arguments in different ways. The forms of the novel and of the literary sentence have been created by established writers, who are mostly men. That most writers have been men is due to the economic and domestic situation of women, argues Woolf.

If there are few great women artists we can think of, this is partly due, she believes, not to the fact that women can't write or paint (think of Lily Briscoe in *To the Lighthouse*), but that women's economic status in the past meant they did not own property, or their own bodies, spent much of their time literally confined domestically, and were not often educated to a standard which would enable them to be original artists and writers.

SHAKESPEARE'S SISTER AND MARY CARMICHAEL

Some modern twentieth-century feminist literary criticism began by rescuing hidden women writers from obscurity and acknowledging that their work was less likely to receive critical attention, less likely to be published than that of their male counterparts. Woolf's views made major contributions to these debates. She developed two examples: Shakespeare's (fictional) sister Judith, and a woman named Mary Carmichael. Shakespeare's sister, she argued, had she existed and had she started out potentially as talented as her famous brother, would never have made it to the London stage and our literary histories because of her poverty, her biology, and the lack of freedom women suffered. She simply would not have had the opportunities to write the plays and see them performed. Mary Carmichael could only write if left some money by an Aunt. From this argument about women's economic position and social silencing, she developed the scenario of having 500 pounds a year and a room of one's own. With these, Woolf argued, you would be able to write, if you had the talent, privacy and some funding.

WOMEN WRITE DIFFERENTLY TO MEN

Woolf's other argument is that women are not only historically prevented from writing, but that they want to and must write in different ways from men. This is more controversial because we do, after all, share the same language. Woolf is one of the very first writers to point out that many words are gendered and carry a sense of being masculine rather than feminine. Sentence constructions even, she argues, can be heavy and pompous, logically organised and built structurally in ways which seem to deny some of the fluidities and balanced views and choices which women are possibly more likely to make. These sorts of views can be expressed in writing which is itself more fluid, less logical and organised. Finally, some women will want to look at life differently, see different images, look at relationships and interactions rather than strict definitions and action-packed adventures. There has been an imbalance in writing so that so many people's versions of life, of language and expression have been denied and undervalued, she argues.

> It is still true that before a woman can write exactly as she wishes to write, she has many difficulties to face. To begin with, there is the technical difficulty – so simple apparently; in reality, so baffling – that the very form of the sentence does not fit her. It is a sentence made by men; it is too loose, too heavy, too pompous for a woman's use.
>
> (Woolf, 'Women and Fiction'. *The Forum*. 1928)

She is not insisting that women's writing is better than men's. Instead, she is pointing out that women's experiences and expression have been missing from writing or downgraded and the balance needs to be redressed.

OPPOSITIONS AND POLARITIES

Woolf's arguments about gender differences also relate to her perceptions about the rigidities of the world view and the dangers of philosophical arguments which insist on dividing the world into oppositions, either/or, black/white. In a world where difference leads to hierarchy and differentiation, there are inevitably going to be boundaries, and boundary disputes. Insistence on polarities, on oppositions, on divisions and hierarchies, leads to a pecking order in which one half of each equation loses out. These oppositions include male/female, active/passive, good/bad, white/black. In these logical polar opposites women, black, bad and passive come out on one side of the equation, the losing side. Such restrictive logic and hierarchising of differences leads directly to imperialism and boundary disputes, and to military conflict. This kind of divisiveness appears in several of her characters who typically deny and prevent difference, see only one choice of action, refuse to accept others' different versions and thus, narrow, define and destroy. Sir William Bradshaw is like this in *Mrs Dalloway*, as is his wife. Mr Ramsay has those tendencies also and it is such rigidities which lead to war, and to the deaths of so many young men, reported off stage in both *Mrs Dalloway*, in the 'Time Passing section' of *To The Lighthouse*, and in *Jacob's Room* where the wastage of war leaves us with only Jacob's boots. As a woman writer, Woolf takes a philosophical stance, pointing out the silencing and absence of women from the higher education academy due to economic restrictions and oppressive social protocol, and argues that such division between the genders is absurd. She goes on to set out an argument that women need to redress this imbalance and that the different subject matters, different thought processes, different language and expression which women bring to writing, should be recognised as equally valid as those of more conventional or traditional writers, who happen for economic reasons to be mostly men. Her arguments made an enormous contribution to the early days of feminist criticism.

NO MORE ANGELS IN THE HOUSE

Woolf argued that, in order to write freely, creatively and critically, she had to exorcise the lingering presence of a Victorian ideal female figure, the Angel in the House (from a poem by Coventry Patmore).

Sometimes the angels would steal her pen.

In this limiting 'ideal' version of women there is no space for creativity or difference, only an idolised perfect mother and wife figure, very ornamental, very static. In her essay 'Professions for Women' she has to rid herself of this phantom presence which prevents her honest writing:

> I discovered that if I were going to review books I should need to do battle with a certain phantom. And the phantom was a woman, and when I came to know her better I called her after the heroine of a famous poem, The Angel in the House. It was she who used to come between me and my paper when I was writing reviews. It was she who bothered me and wasted my time and so tormented me that at last I killed her... I will describe her as shortly as I can. She was intensely sympathetic. She was immensely charming. She was utterly unselfish. She excelled in the difficult arts of family life. She sacrificed herself daily. If there was a chicken, she took the leg; if there was a draught she sat in it – in short she was so constituted that she never had a mind or a wish of her own but preferred to sympathise always with the minds and wishes of others.
>
> (essay 'Professions for Women – The Death of the Moth').

Partly, this figure reminds her of her nurturing mother, who appears in *To the Lighthouse* in the figure of Mrs Ramsay.

A Room of One's Own.

Virginia Woolf's arguments about the economic situation of women artists and writers is developed fully in the long essay 'A Room of One's Own', based on lectures she gave at Girton and Newnham, the two women's colleges of the University of Cambridge. One of her comments about how women's writing has been treated highlights the comparison between men's writing – which tends to be about war or politics – and women's writing which is often dismissed because its subject matter is different:

> This is an insignificant book because it deals with the feelings of women in a drawing-room. A scene in a battlefield is more important than a scene in a shop.

> *(Ibid)*

For the woman writer, one's versions of life must be skewed to fit what is considered important. Women actually need to write with different rhythms, images and language if they really want to express themselves and their lives because:

The weight, the pace, the stride of a man's mind are too unlike her for her to lift anything substantial from him successfully.

(Ibid)

Woolf argues that in order for a woman to write, the shape of the novel also needs changing, as does that of the sentence.

Woolf 'rescued' women from history, and herself wrote critical comments on the women writers of her time and previous ages – notably on Emily Brontë as a poet, and Dorothy Richardson as a novelist. Co-running the Hogarth Press enabled her to publish her own work and that of other women and men, and she also published the work of the Women's Cooperative (working class women).

Part of Woolf's innovation in terms of style is her deliberate (pre) feminist development: the flexibility of the sentences, the focus on the stream of consciousness, the inner self and relationships; all these things reflect women's experiences which have been hidden from literature, and enable a feminised representation of both women's and men's experiences. So some of her challenge as a woman to the literary establishment and to the language and form of the novel is pure experimentation in itself as well as a proto or pre-feminist exploration.

MODERNIST CHALLENGES TO THE NOVEL

New ways of writing

Woolf wanted to capture and express life, reality, feelings, thoughts, relationships, the passing of time: the different ways in which we make sense of the world, of other people and of ourselves. More traditional novelists have tried to do this too, of course, but their choices are more likely to be in line with the **realist novel** than are Woolf's. Woolf, like other innovative writers influenced by her and the

> **KEY TERM**
>
> Realist novel A term particularly associated with the nineteenth century novel to refer to the idea that texts appear to represent the world *as it really is.*

other modernists (James Joyce, for example, another great modernist) refused the nineteenth century novel's mode of realism and instead concentrated on representing life as they felt it to be *experienced*.

Her most famous exploration of this state of experience and expression appears in the essay 'Modern Fiction':

> The writer seems constrained, not by his own free will, but by some powerful and unscrupulous tyrant who has him in thrall, to pro-vide a plot, to provide comedy, tragedy, love interest, and an air of probability embalming the whole so impeccably that if all his figures were to come to life they would find themselves dressed down to the last button of their coats in the fashion of the hour.

> Look within and life, it seems, is very far from being 'like this'. Examine for a moment an ordinary mind on an ordinary day. The mind receives a myriad impressions – trivial, fantastic, evanescent, or engraved with the sharpness of steel. From all sides they come, an incessant shower of innumerable atoms; and as they fall, as they shape themselves into the life of Monday or Tuesday, the accent falls differently from of old; the moment of importance came not here but there; so that if a writer were a free man and not a slave, if he could write what he chose, not what he must, if he could base his work upon his own feeling and not upon convention, there would be no plot, no comedy, no tragedy, no love interest or catastrophe in the accepted style, and perhaps not a single button sewn on as the Bond Street tailors would have it. Life is not a series of gig lamps symmetrically arranged; life is a luminous halo, a semi-transparent envelope surrounding us from the beginning of consciousness in the end.

> (essay 'Modern Fiction')

Subjectivity of experience

Reality is, Woolf asserts, something which we each perceive differently, so presenting people and events as if everyone experienced them in the same way, and all the time, in a non-objective manner, would actually not capture reality, real events, real people at all. Human experiences and relationships changed in the new century, she argued, influenced by Freud, Jung, Marx, and new technologies as well as the advent of war. In the light of such changes, human relations changed and new forms of expression needed to be sought to express this. She picks an arbitrary date (ironically) for such changes: 'In or about December 10, human nature changed. ... And when human relations change, there is at the same time a change in religion, conduct, politics and literature.' ('Mr Bennett and Mrs Brown').

Woolf's development of a very different technique to that familiar in the more conventional nineteenth- and early twentieth-century novelist was, therefore, partly a response to her opinion, (as that of other writers), that the world itself had changed enormously. Writing needed to reflect that change, in order to capture it.

In challenging what she termed the tyrants of the novel, Woolf worked to reflect felt and lived reality. This she partly did through the use of 'stream of consciousness'. What follows is writing which captures what philosophers call sense impressions – our sense of smell, sound, touch, hearing. It also captures thought patterns that often appear in symbols, rhythms and images, and yet have to be translated in words to make any sense to the thinker. Like the French writer and philosopher, Bergson, Woolf also felt that time, our inner sense of time passing, needed to be expressed other than in a rigidly chronological fashion with events and changes marked discreetly. Events which are close together, she felt, must influence the present, the present must influence the future and so on.

Additionally, we all experience a sense of the flow of time differently in different contexts. For example, in the opening pages of *Mrs Dalloway*, Clarissa runs together her memories of Ourton, where she stayed as a younger woman; thoughts of Peter Walsh's return; and the present day, when she is preparing her party. Her sense of smell, hearing and her feelings from the past run together with, and are triggered off by, her feelings and experience in the present. Mrs Ramsay, in *To the Lighthouse*, sinking down after the dinner party has finished, feels that time has no boundaries, and neither does space. She feels it moves very slowly, and she could travel anywhere, be anything. This registers 'inner time'.

Later in the twentieth century, a school of writers in France called the Nouveau Roman school – Robbe Grillet, Nathalie Sarraute and others – took stream of consciousness much further and concentrated on *sous* conversations or sub conversations. These are thoughts we have before we fully put them into a form to share with others. This acknowledges that in trying to capture thoughts and feelings, the writer, however innovative, inevitably has to shape and choose words. These words are always only a stab at expressing the feelings, but nonetheless, a stab which others can start to share and understand.

So the stream of consciousness is not an unmediated stream; usually the flow of someone's thoughts are cut into by a disembodied narrator who points out how someone is feeling, what they are now doing. The thoughts most often appear first with actions following, or subsidiary thoughts following. This emphasises how Woolf felt that actually, our experiences are really individualised and subjective. When Mrs Ramsay sits everyone down to dinner, for example, we have first her thoughts, then her words and actions. In her thoughts she feels weary, as if her life has produced nothing, while her words to others are quite directing, though the tiredness attaching to them springs straight-forwardly from her feeling of personal life weariness:

'But what have I done with my life?' thought Mrs Ramsay, taking her place at the head of the table, and looking at all the plates making white circles on it. 'William, sit by me,' she said, 'Lily,' she said wearily, 'over there.' they had that-Paul Rayley and Minta Doyle-she, only this – an infinitely long table and plates and knives. At the far end, was her husband, sitting down all in a heap, frowning. What at? She did not know. She did not mind.

This piece is also quite amusing. Literally, her weariness translates into seeing only the endless table with plates and cutlery – a very solid, concrete, domestic example. And her husband is frowning, but she cannot see into his thoughts, and neither can we – but we can imagine some endless piece of self-related sorrow is troubling him – he cannot be a social being.

She also develops a kind of **shared subjectivity** or intersubjectivity. In her use of this form she explores the ways in which, in coming together, we all form a shared experience, change our views of each other, move on, come to some conclusions, and change them again. The moment for a family or a group of friends or acquaintances is made unique because it is shared. Moving around the feelings, emotions, experiences and points of view of several people she can explore and dramatise this. This is really a very innovative technique and also, it could be argued, a very female one since Woolf is being deliberately social and deliberately uniting people, representing how they make an experience and share it.

> **KEY FACT**
>
> Shared subjectivity or intersubjectivity In her use of this form Virginia Woolf explores the ways in which, in coming together at parties, dinners, in the street, talking or just being together, we all form a shared experience, change our views of each other, move on, come to some conclusions, and change them again.

In *To the Lighthouse* for instance, the sharing of a meal captures the different responses people have to each other. One moment Mrs

Ramsay feels irritated by William Bankes, the next she feels sorry for him as he has not married, and gives him a particularly good portion of the food. Then she feels supportive of the young couple Paul and Minta, and determined they should become an established pair, and then worried about them. Her moods, responses, the slant she puts on the interactions between them on all, the shape of the moment, move around and differ. Different people round the table are also consulted by this roving narrative point of view and we then move inside the feelings of other characters who are feeling part of the scene or left out, wondering about various developments, criticising (Charles Tansley does this a great deal) or trying to fit in. And Woolf moves us from person to person. She captures the ways in which each individual thinks and changes their thoughts not merely by **interior monologue**, but also by narrating the story, by describing the scene using the kinds of phrases and images that a particular person would use.

KEYWORD

Interior monologue The voice speaking to you about what you are doing inside your head. It is a flow of thoughts expressed as words, with sentences usually starting 'I ...' and is a kind of commentary on how someone is feeling and what they are experiencing.

So the flow is not jerking from a character's thoughts to another's, but smooth and in what would be called in Jane Austen's novels, 'free indirect speech' (see page 10). It is the adopting of different kinds of language and expressions to describe what a character is doing or to represent their feelings, that forms a shared experience.

Woolf enables us to be more broad-minded, and to see there are many points of view. Nothing is entirely fixed and limited. Her work is structured, but flexible, and while different feelings are articulated, they are also shown as larger and less clearly defined than the words which try to capture them, more varied than agreements about shared experience and labels.

IDENTITY AND RELATIONSHIPS

Separateness of the self

One of Woolf's major concerns is the search for identity, for the self. Her characters often have a rather tenuous sense of identity, feeling that they play roles, don and wear clothes and behaviours, but that there is somehow another self hidden away, separate from this role-playing, social self. In medical terms, this could be termed schizophrenia and in the characters who have depressive incidents, or who commit suicide, like Rhoda in *The Waves* or Septimus Warren Smith in *Mrs Dalloway*, a medical reading of their psychological condition is probably quite correct. But Woolf also takes what became a very popular stance about women and sensitive individuals' feelings of identity and relationship to reality. In the 1960s and beyond, writers such as Doris Lessing (*Briefing for a Descent into Hell, The Summer Before the Dark, The Golden Notebook*) explored the kind of separateness of the individual self from the self enacted as a set of roles in the shared social world. The psychoanalyst R.D. Laing also wrote about breakdown as being a kind of potential breakthrough, and the American novelist Ken Kesey's *One Flew Over the Cuckoo's Nest* questioned definitions of conformity and sanity. Feeling separate as a self from the social world, questioning what seems to be commonly accepted as reality, is a position which is not only radical but imaginative, creative and positive. Woolf, we know, had periods of depression and even 'madness'. However, there have been many critics who have related her breakdowns to overwork. More fundamentally, perhaps, they can be understood as a clash between the values, feelings and experience she had as a woman and a writer, and those she seemed to be expected to have in a world which was run along very patriarchal lines. Her world view seemed undermined and changed by the dominant ideology which was patriarchy.

For Rachel Vinrace in *The Voyage Out* the sense of loss of reality, of floating, is one which only emerges when she is delirious. Woolf characterises such a sinking down not as one that frees up possibilities and questions about dignity and reality, but as a threat. In *The Waves*, Rhoda has a similar fate. Her suicide is a direct result of her tenuous hold on what could be described as a shared reality. Losing a sense of identity, Rhoda feels threatened by spaces and things; the puddles seem to hold potential holes to suck her in, the sheets holes to let her through. Mrs Ramsay frequently sinks down into herself and speculates about roles, structures and the rules of life. Hers is not a sense of total dissolution but she aligns herself with the rhythms of nature and the stroke of the lighthouse. Her mind wanders onto possible alternative lives, onto the meaning of life.

Woolf has a keen sense of how people misunderstand, resent and irritate each other.

THE PERSONAL IS POLITICAL: PUBLIC AND PRIVATE

Woolf's work embraces both the personal and the political, the public and the private. Although it might be popular for some critics to claim that her intense concentration on the flow of thoughts and experiences, the 'atoms as they fall' means that she is an inner-gazing novelist, nevertheless Woolf is also a writer who places her characters very much within the lived moment, the historical context and in public spaces. Additionally, she is a forerunner of what the mid-twentieth century women's movement started to use as its slogan – 'the personal is political'. In personal lives and feelings, Woolf explores the politics of economic power, male/female relations and the oppressive patriarchal world view which led people to be so divisive, to take difference as a reason for destruction as well as hierarchy. This philosophical belief led, as we have seen, in her view and in that of many subsequent feminists, (Julia Kristeva, for example) to war and destruction. Woolf encourages the women of the women's co-operative movement to write and publish their life stories. She also writes acutely unpleasant and very critically astute reviews of other great writers. Hers was a comfortable life, but she was not quite the elitist that she seems. Her political engagement was not of the activist sort, but philosophical and through her writing, notably linking economics and women's equality in 'A Room of One's Own' and the rigid world view of patriarchy which led to disastrous deaths in the First World War in 'Three Guineas'. Anna Snaith's work (2000) explores Woolf's treatment of public and private spaces much further.

KEY FACT

French feminists: Julia Kristeva, Helene Cixous, Luce Irigaray. The French Feminist thinkers and critics of the 1970s onwards have been influenced by and develop their thoughts further than the French psychoanalytical critic, Jaqcues Lacan, himself a follower of the work of Sigmund Freud.

Helene Cixous argues, in 'The Laugh of the Medusa', that the world has been seen as split into binary opposites good/bad, black/white, male /female, self/other and that this rigid polarising way of looking at things causes divisions, hostilities, the development of territorial behaviours, hierarchies, boundaries and then war. Woolf says much the same thing in her *Three Guineas* and in her notions of combining the qualities of both sexes in androgyny. Cixous also talks about the fluidity and flexibility of women's writing which captures moods and flow, is creative and organic.

Julia Kristeva comments, in '*Strangers to Ourselves*', on how we need not reject others because they are different from us, but to recognise that we tend to place onto other people those elements of ourselves which we can't quite come to terms with. The dislike or hatred tends to come from within. We need to recognise the other in ourselves. She also has a notion of 'woman's time' which she says is not bound to rigid chronology, but is time as it is felt.

Luce Irigaray writes, in *The Newly Born Woman*, about the importance of the relationships between the mother and child, about women and their bodies being an important felt connection not to be ignored.

✳✳✳✳SUMMARY ✳✳✳✳

- Woolf's writing was experimental and innovative. It examined roles for women and representations of women.

- She uses different writing techniques, subject matter and imagery to suit women writers, and readers.

- As a literary modernist, Woolf used and developed the technique of 'stream of consciousness', of interior monologue, free indirect speech, symbolism and intersubjectivity – and experimentation generally.

- Woolf's interest in exploring the self, reality, identity and relationships is apparent in all her work.

5 Major Works

GENERAL

Virginia Woolf is mainly famous for her novels, but she also wrote short stories and critical essays, both on the situation of women and writing, and on the work of other writers. Looking at her earlier work provides insights into the later, better known novels. Her greatest works *Mrs Dalloway* (1925) and *To the Lighthouse* (1927) break new ground in terms of challenging the conventional characteristics of the novel.

MRS DALLOWAY (1925)

Mrs Dalloway is ostensibly a novel about an upper middle class woman, Clarissa Dalloway (based on a society hostess Woolf knew). Having recovered from the deadly flu which claimed so many lives, she considers her situation in life, decides she has the energy to keep living, and prepares and throws a party. This is the plot, but actually the novel is much more about states of consciousness, choices between life and death, as well as about the terrible effects of the First World War on people's lives. It is, then, both a historically contextualised novel which looks at a particular time period – just after the First World War – and a particular place – London. It is also a novel that explores a new sense of reality, concentrating on how people feel, change their minds, mix memory with sense impressions and thoughts of the future. It explores the kinds of inner thoughts they have while simultaneously saying and doing things in the social world. It is in expressing these changing experiences, this individuality, these inner thoughts that Woolf is so technically innovative. With Mrs Dalloway we have her first really completely experimental novel.

A day in the life of Clarissa Dalloway
The all-seeing eye
The story takes place during one day only. This in itself unites the characters, but Virginia Woolf takes pains to show that, in traditional fiction, the imposition of the form of an incident, rounded off, holding a few chosen characters in it, is a very artificial way of representing life. She shows other links. At any moment, people are united by experiencing the same event, be it the striking of Big Ben, the flying overhead of an aeroplane, the travelling through a crowd of a car bearing an important and unknown person. When representing these incidents which unite people, the narrating voice is frequently not that of Clarissa's thoughts, but a sort of disembodied, ever-present spirit: a narrating 'eye' which sees all. This narrating, all-seeing 'eye' is another of her innovations in the novel – she does not intrude as author but produces a narrating voice perceiving and expressing everything.

The novel ends with a party. Clarissa, hostess, is successfully organising people, particularly proud to have the Prime Minister, representative of male organisation and success in the world, at her party.

Stream of consciousness and technical experimentation
In *Mrs Dalloway* Virginia Woolf uses stream of consciousness fully for the first time. The experience of Clarissa in particular is presented to us by the thoughts that run through her mind. Each moment is a mixture of sensations, memories, hopes and fears, every experience is coloured by the sensations of the moment, affected by the past and thoughts of the future. Characters are shown to us through their thoughts and changing ideas of themselves, and the thoughts others have of them.

Time
Time is very important in this novel as a structuring device, and it is also used to represent different kinds of awareness, both objective and subjective. There are two sorts of time, the clock time of Big Ben in particular – chronological, ordered time, and **inner time** or '**Durée**' (page 36) as the French philosopher and writer, Henri Bergson, labelled it.

Mrs Dalloway's thoughts wrapped her world.

Throughout the novel we are constantly reminded of the time, and shown how 'inner time' differs. While Big Ben strikes throughout the novel and represents ordered time, external reality, another clock also strikes, representing a more creative, different, less marked and less fixed inner time. St Margaret's, the London church, has a clock which strikes in a less definite way, more hesitant, like a hostess entering a room, less eager to impress itself definitely on others, less ordered. The striking of this clock is compared to the actions of Clarissa Dalloway which are less dominant and incisive than those of other characters in the novel such as Lady Bruton, Miss Kilman and Sir William Bradshaw the doctor.

KEY TERM

Inner time or 'Duree' The sensation of time we feel personally, the feeling that things are going slowly when we are bored, quickly when we are excited for example, and the loss of all sense of external time we have when we sink into ourselves and just think.

Clarissa Dalloway and Septimus Warren Smith
Clarissa

The juxtaposition of the lives of the two central characters, Clarissa Dalloway and Septimus Warren Smith, is used by Woolf as a structuring device within the novel. Clarissa has sacrificed the excitement and love she could have had with Peter Walsh for a 'narrow bed'. She is frequently described in chaste nun images. But she has the ability to keep a part of herself to herself, in her rather loveless marriage with Richard Dalloway. Her achievements are all social; she gives successful parties like the one she is preparing for and gives in the novel. This side to Clarissa copes with life and orders it, acts in the world. Like so many of Woolf's female characters, she is creative socially.

The other side to Clarissa longs for easeful death and with it a union with something that outlasts man, and is eternal perhaps. She says we are not fully understood by others, that we act roles in the shared social world, but our inner selves are never fully fixed or revealed. This leads to a sense of being isolated and locked in one's self. It also suggests aligning the individual with everything that exists, with nature. With one half of herself Clarissa can give successful parties and charm her guest, the Prime Minister, while the other half wishes to opt out of the bustle. This other half is fully acted out in Septimus Warren Smith, a First World War shell-shock victim, whose thoughts occupy a large part of the novel.

Septimus

External reality, the objective world as experienced by the majority of people, is strange to Septimus Smith, lost in his own subjective world. He can act out instincts suppressed in Clarissa, withdrawing into a dream world that frequently seems more like a nightmare. He sees dead friends in Regent's Park and hears the birds talk in Greek.

Septimus Smith feels a oneness with nature and desires a dissolution. He is described with Woolf's familiar watery imagery, as a 'drowned sailor'. Evocations of his madness have been seen as based on Woolf's own periods of madness. They are nearer to poetry than prose in their rhythms and imagery. He feels beauty and terror but chooses dissolution. Significantly, the doctors who see Smith don't understand him at all, lack sympathy and imagination. In her description of Sir William Bradshaw, Virginia Woolf steps into the novel as intrusive narrator for the only time, and drives home a strong condemnation. She is condemning that world which demands that one must conform to rules that everyone must be and think alike and see the world alike.

Sir William Bradshaw is seen as a worshipper of Proportion and Conversion:

> Worshipping Proportion, Sir William not only prospered himself but made England prosper! Secluded her lunatics, forbade childbirth, penalised despair, made it impossible for the unfit to propagate their views until they too shared his sense of proportion... but Proportion had a sister, less smiling, more formidable, a Goddess even now engaged – in the heat and sands of India, the mud and swamp of Africa, the purlieus of London, wherever, in short, the climate or the devil tempts men to fall from the true belief which is her own – is even now engaged in dashing down shrines, smashing idols, and setting up in their place her own stern countenance. Conversion is her name and she feasts on the wills of the weakly, loving to impress, to impose, adoring her own features stamped on the face of the populace.... But conversion, fastidious Goddess, loves blood better than brick and feasts most subtly on the human will.

These controlling, tyrannical doctors are based on the doctors Woolf herself suffered under, who prescribed bed rest and thought her mad.

Clarissa chooses life

Smith's story unites with Clarissa's at her party, since she hears of his suicide. She feels in a way that his choice of death is an escape. He has, though, taken from her the burden of whether to seek dissolution herself or not; she chooses life. She is saved by his actions, and feels 'a thing there was that mattered; a thing, weathered about with chatter, defaced, obscured in her own life, let drop every day in lies, corruption, chatter. This he has preserved'. He has made a choice. Death seems appealing 'Death was defiance. ... Death was an attempt to communicate. ... There was an embrace in Death.' But, then she thinks about the importance of life, companionship, action, relationships.

Because he has chosen death something is resolved in her. She feels revived, happy, she does not have to choose death herself, he has done it for her. And in characteristic gesture, she plunges into life – and her party.

Women's lives

The different versions of women's lives explored in the novel indicate Woolf's recognition of the constructions and possibilities open to women in her day. While she critiques the repressive limited world view of the doctor, Sir William Bradshaw, showing his version of conformity and reason to be deadening, she does not simply set positive versions of women against negative versions of men. Both Lady Bradshaw, Sir William's wife, and Miss Kilman are women whose lives are rigid. Miss Kilman has intellectual control over Elizabeth, Mrs Dalloway's daughter.

Clarissa Dalloway remembers her youth as a girl entering the social world, beginning to form relationships, and recalls how she fell in love with both Peter Walsh and Sally Seton. Sally represents a different kind of woman to Clarissa, one who has more freedom. Clarissa recalls:

> But all that evening she could not take her eyes off Sally. It was an extraordinary beauty of the kind she most admired, dark, large-eyed,

with that quality which, since she hadn't got it herself, she always envied – a sort of abandonment, as if she could say anything, do anything; a quality much commoner in foreigners that in Englishwomen.

Elizabeth Dalloway has more opportunities than Clarissa, or Rachel in *The Voyage Out*. In the section where Elizabeth boards the bus, she is described as an 'impetuous pirate' (p.151). She responds freely to the movements of the bus 'like a rider, like the figure-head of a ship', and she goes wherever she pleases – to the Strand, and beyond if she likes. A young woman in the early part of the century after the war, Elizabeth's choices are many.

Mrs Dalloway concentrates on many of Woolf's favourite themes – identity, relationships, the role of women and possibilities for women, and sanity, perception. These themes are taken up further in *To the Lighthouse*.

TO THE LIGHTHOUSE (1925)

What happens in To the Lighthouse?

To the Lighthouse is about life, time passing, people coming together, influencing each other, misunderstanding and attempting to understand each other, relating or not relating to one other. It concerns interactions. It is about people having different individualistic responses to the same shared event, changing their minds regularly and instantly about people and events and experiences. It is about the passage over time for a family in their country home by the sea. The first and third sections concentrate on the family, the Ramsays, and their friends, at their holiday home. The central section 'Time Passes' focuses on the house while no-one is there. While the first and third sections only cover a few days, this central section lasts for ten years. For the family, one of their intentions is to complete the voyage to the lighthouse which was promised but not fulfilled in the first section. The trip to the lighthouse is a kind of emotional pilgrimage.

The book also concerns questions about what lasts and whether it is possible for us to leave behind a trace of our existence. Philosophy, writing, art, all are suggested as possibilities here, and at the centre of the novel in addition to the Ramsays is Lily Briscoe, an artist. Lily attempts to capture her feelings of reality and of experience throughout her first visit to the house on the island. When she returns, she manages to do so, and finishes her picture. This takes place at the same time as the remainder of the family arrive at the lighthouse and so both events provide an artistic resolution to the book.

But of course, it is hard to sum up its plot, for plot is one of the enemies of the novel in Woolf's work!

Mr and Mrs Ramsay – versions of life and relationships

Mr and Mrs Ramsay are juxtaposed as characters and as representatives of different ways of seeing the world. Mr Ramsay has a logical mind, believes he can sort existence into categories and boxes. He thinks 'If thought is like the keyboard of a piano, divided into so many notes....' He is trying in his philosophical speculation to reach ultimate truths represented here as a struggle. Earlier thoughts in this logical progression are seen as P and Q. These are terms used in philosophical reasoning, but here they are also ironised, because Mr Ramsay's version of seeking truth is absurdly logical and literal, seeing the seeking of understanding as a linear activity moving from one difficult thought on and on through more difficult thoughts until everything, eventually, will be understood. Woolf is ironising the highly logical mind, which depends on reason and feels everything can be understood. It can't, she suggests, and going about understanding life this way will only lead to frustration. Life is too diverse and flexible and too different to be so caught.

Mr Ramsay lacks warmth and intuition but he constantly demands sympathy from his wife, draining her energies. As she responds to him she seems to: 'pour erect into the air a rain of energy, a column of spray'.

Mr and Mrs Ramsay see the world totally differently. She is an 'earth mother', sensitive, intuitive and emotional, and has a very subjective approach, while he is cold and logical and tries to be objective. This is illustrated when they look at their flowers. To him they are just a categorisable colour, while she is reminded by looking at the flowers how she required them to be planted. She feels differently about them, feels involved and warm towards them. Woolf uses the flowers realistically and symbolically. They are real flowers, after all they can be seen by both husband and wife, and yet they are symbolical, their colours representing the different ways in which Mr and Mrs Ramsay appreciate life itself.

Philosophical questions in the novel

The novel throws up some of the big questions in life. Mr Ramsay needs to know what it is of us that lasts? Why do people bother to create, act, think? What really remains? The Ramsays themselves and other couples in Woolf's work force us to question how much we can ever know each other (and whether this matters). Both Augustus Carmichael and Lily Briscoe, in different ways (like Mr Ramsay) ask questions about how art might try and imagine and represent life and how it can cast light and some sense of structure on it. An impression is preferable to having life forced onwards, subservient to the force of nature, pointless, brutalised.

The central part of the novel, 'Time Passes', presents us with these questions and works towards some suggestions. It depicts for us nature, a house containing memories, where no-one lives and where nothing remains but a lingering memory and impression. Brutalised, unthinking, insensitive experience is captured in the complete absence of human life, the assertion of nature with no direction. This central section of the novel is the most experimental and innovative. It throws all we do into relief, because the spotlight is put onto nature *without* humankind. In this section, Woolf also returns some human order, finally, and seems to suggest that humankind can act intelligently, convey meaning, even if it is only a construction over the chaos of sheer existence, nature red in tooth and claw: insensitive, unintelligent.

Mr Ramsay fears that his books will disappear with time. It will be as if he never existed, except that he has provided the world with so many children. He takes consolation in the fact that the works of Sir Walter Scott and Shakespeare have survived. And indeed, Mr Ramsay's books do survive the onslaught of nature when the house is left empty over many years. Towards the end of 'Time Passes' the cleaners return and sort out the house, laying damp things to dry on the lawn and rescuing Mr Ramsay's books.

Another answer to the question 'what lasts?' is found in the continually felt presence of Mrs Ramsay even after her death. The influence of strong personalities lasts on in those who remain, and Lily Briscoe even feels that she sees Mrs Ramsay again, sitting with James in the doorway. Her lingering presence enables people to finally come together and finish some of their projects.

Lily Briscoe, Mrs Ramsay and the role of women

To the Lighthouse investigates a variety of roles for women. There are two main female characters in the novel, Mrs Ramsay and Lily Briscoe, with Nancy and Prue, and Minta Doyle, representing other examples of women's roles and choices.

Woolf, in recreating her mother, Julia Stephen, in Mrs Ramsay, pays her homage. She also, however, needs to exorcise the power her mother had over her. It would be impossible, under the eyes of such selflessness and yet such an emotional control, to actually get on with painting or writing. Women, Mrs Ramsay believes, are there to care for others, harmonise everyone, marry people off, and be protected by men. They are also there to protect men, to nurture their egos, not disagree in public, and to smooth over awkward moments.

> She had the whole of the other sex under her protection; for reasons she could not explain, for their chivalry and valour, for the fact that they negotiated treaties, ruled India, controlled finance.

Mrs Ramsay is an ideal kind of nurturer. She has six children and loves organising their lives and harmonising people. She is an artist in life, constantly aware of people's feelings so that she can care for them, say what is needed. She is depicted in images of green, wrapped in a green shawl, a symbol of fertility. She gets her bearings by the trees outside and responds to nature.

When she organises the dinner party at which all friends and family eat *bœuf en daube*, Mrs Ramsay feels she has created a moment out of time which, because it is perfect, an artwork in human relations, will last and be remembered. Indeed, her memory lingers on in the holiday home when she has died. When Lily later sees her and James, her son, in a visionary moment, this enables Lily to complete her picture. But Lily Briscoe herself actually represents a very different kind of woman, and in creating this figure Woolf is investigating the variety of experiences and doors open to women, the constraints and the possibilities. Even though she is successful as an artist, Lily herself feels both strong as an individual and somehow lacking, rather in awe of the centralising figure of Mrs Ramsay. This shows the strength of the representation of versions of women that Mrs Ramsay epitomises – the nurturing Madonna.

As an artist, Lily is sensitive about the role of women and feels constantly pressurised by Mrs Ramsay into bolstering male egos. Mrs Ramsay obviously wills her to be polite to Charlie Tansley, the sceptical follower of Mr Ramsay, yet she finds it hard and feels she is betraying her own nature to so abase herself. Tansley really does not like women, can see no point to them:

> It was the women's fault. Women made civilisation impossible with all their 'charm', all their silliness.

The draining effect Lily feels when she is expected to bolster up Tansley is also connected with the sensation she has when he is around that he is constantly deprecating her work. 'Women can't write, women can't paint', she can hear him say, and it makes her creative springs dry up totally. The same happens when, in the last section, Mr Ramsay comes to Lily, now that his wife is dead, to provide the sympathy which he feels is the woman's role to provide for a man. This self-sacrifice drains women of energy and prevents them from painting or doing anything creative. Lily feels both that she can't and won't give sympathy, must keep herself inviolate emotionally or she can't create, which is her life, and yet that in some way she is being less than a woman by refusing to sympathise. She feels others must think her a dried up old spinster when she can't respond:

> But let him be fifty feet away, let him not even speak to you, let him not even see you, he permeated, he prevailed, he imposed himself. He changed everything. She could not see the colour; she could not see the lines; even with his back to her she could only think – But he'll be down on me in a moment, demanding – something she felt she could not give him.

In the final section, Lily takes over as the main experiencing consciousness through whose feelings and sensations everything is centred. She is very like Mrs Ramsay in being sensitive and intuitive rather than logical, as Mr Ramsay is. She is in fact unable to really imagine objects and the nature of reality. When she asks one of the children about what his father Mr Ramsay is working on, it turns out also to be about the nature of reality, but perceived in a very philosophical and logical way.

Woolf's technique
Stream of consciousness, symbolism
Woolf's style in *To the Lighthouse* highlights the difficulties we have in pinning relationships and experience down. She shows how a mind flits from thought to thought, sensation to sensation and constantly makes different assessments of self and others. There are also many comments, particularly from the astute Lily.

One wanted fifty pairs of eyes to see with...fifty pairs of eyes were not enough to get round that one woman with, she thought' and 'Half one's notions of other people were after all grotesque. They served private purposes of one's own.'

This method of representing different ways in which we perceive others – according to time, place, mood and people's actions, and how we change this perception in different contexts, so that we can never *really* know each other or fix our own responses – is very like the art movement called **Post Impressionism**. This movement was

Virginia Woolf as Cubist portrait.

contemporary with Woolf and the modernists. At the same time, Cubism and the work of Picasso were also gaining importance, and Picasso's *les demoiselles d'avignon* for example, provides a Cubist rendering of women seen from several different angles at once. This suggests that we have many facets, and while such a painting gives us these facets visually, the literary work, in particular that of Woolf, renders these facets and interpretations through free indirect speech symbols. Woolf's techniques evoke how people and events are perceived, and how these perceptions change with time and context.

KEY TERM

Post Impressionism an artistic movement in which the whole is made up of many different elements in different colours, and seen from a distance it forms a certain shape, a different picture to that seen up close.

Identity and self: experimental techniques

This novel is notable also for the ways in which it represents people's thoughts, their sense of identity and how that can change. Mrs Ramsay removes herself from the hustle and bustle of the social scenes she creates and tries to search for a sense of self elsewhere.

Consider the scene where she is resting after the dinner party towards the end of the first section. Notice that her thoughts are constantly interrupted in her mind by other thoughts; every experience is a mixture of sensations, memories, hopes and prejudices. The main body of the narration describes what goes on in Mrs Ramsay's mind, her interior monologue. Comments on what she does or feels are secondary to this, and so are put in brackets.

Although an artist in human life, mother and hostess Mrs Ramsay often feels removed from all this and sinks down into herself, alone. There she feels at one with nature, with eternity, with something that outlasts the moment and goes on forever. This is an important discussion of the inner self which feels removed from the outer reality of society, roles and rules. As her thoughts before the dinner party show, taking part in reality is a definite decision. She is well aware of donning roles and acting in certain ways. This split, taken to extreme, leads to schizophrenia of course, but in Mrs Ramsay it is not problematical at all. She is self aware, and she mixes in the world. One thing which this sinking down into herself does suggest is that she seeks confirmation of what she senses: a life that continues, in nature outside our lives here and now, that lasts forever, i.e as if individuals were part of nature as are all flowers, all living things, not individualised.

Time and memory
Memory is important in the novel, either memory that is used to keep alive a sense of those who have died or memory which acts to constantly colour the way we see the world. Time is also important.

Non-clock time reigns supreme in the central part of the novel, 'Time Passes'. Here the house has been shut up and left, almost to be taken over by nature. Nature and the house are of central interest here so the actions of people and events concerning them such as the war and the deaths of Prue, Andrew and Mrs Ramsay, are all placed in brackets because they are less important. This part is prose poetry, ruled by its own images and rhythms. Gradually nature advances on the things of man:

> So with the house empty and the doors locked and the mattresses rolled away, those stray airs, advance guards of great armies, blustered in, brushed bare boards nibbled and fanned, met nothing in bedroom or drawing room that wholly resisted them but only hangings that flapped, wood that creaked, the bare legs of tables, saucepans and china already furred, tarnished, cracked.

Eventually nature almost takes over completely. This whole section is a marvellous evocation of the energy of nature and its existence completely removed from man. It is eyeless. It exists whether there is man around to experience it or not. Throughout, the beams of the lighthouse rhythmically stroke the house.

Artistic closure – how does the novel end and why?
The novel deals with ways of seeing, with life and death, time and memory, relationships, art and life, and it comes to a final, totally satisfying close. As the boat taking Mr Ramsay, James and Cam to the lighthouse finally reaches its destination, thus completing one of the story lines, so their misunderstandings which have lasted throughout the book cease. At the same time, Lily has had her vision. She has seen Mrs Ramsay as a vision, centralising Lily's own perceptions in her

work, Lily manages to finish the painting she has been working on throughout. The book ends optimistically. People live on after death somehow, as Mrs Ramsay seems to. The ending also provides an artistic completion with all the major themes and story lines completed, an artwork.

ORLANDO (1928)

Orlando is a marvellously amusing novel, and one that undermines many of the things we think are fixed and controlling in life as well as in novels. In *Orlando*, boundaries between the genders are eroded. Orlando is both a young man in the period of Shakespeare's day, the day of the Great Freeze in London, and a woman during the nineteenth and early twentieth century.

Playing with different genders

Orlando walks through time.

Playing with different genders and transgressing genders enables Woolf to try out the answers to several questions. One is to consider what if a talented man in a particular period were actually a woman – what would the social constraints be? What the opportunities? She investigates the questions of gender and power through the changing gender of the androgynous Orlando. She also transgresses the hold that conventions of time have on us in life and novels and has Orlando live for hundreds of years, during which time s/he hardly ages. In this she can explore 'what if' questions: what if a man or a woman were actually living in a different period, what would be possible? who could own land? what freedoms and constraints would there be?

Androgyny and creativity

Orlando represents Woolf working out her theories about the creative imagination being ideally androgynous. She argues that it is best not to emphasise the needs, versions or problems of one gender over the other, but write and create as if gender-free, in the writer's mind having the best of both kinds of experience, insight and expression. Orlando, being both male and female, can use both kinds of writing styles.

Style of Orlando

Orlando also changes his/her writing style and chosen form according to the period in which s/he is writing. So s/he starts off by writing an epic poem, *The Oak Tree*. This work changes form through the centuries becoming by turns a play, a poem and a novel. This answers questions about how literary forms change in order to represent feelings and arguments in the world. The oak tree itself, rooted in the earth, is an Anglo-Saxon idea, that of a great tree at the core of the earth holding everything together. So Orlando is allied to eternal human and earth life in her/his writing. In the questioning of gendered roles and the ways in which clothes, behaviour and society construct us, Woolf shows herself to be a feminist writer and one far ahead of her time.

Gender as a construction

In the latter part of the twentieth century, writers such as Judith Butler have explored the ways in which we are constructed as gendered beings and how culture and society conditions us to wear certain clothes, be constrained in our actions, our opportunities, our speech and our experiences according to gender. By playing with changing gender and changing it, you highlight this. Woolf also shows she has a sense of humour – there are many very funny moments of cross dressing, exposure and even the kind of farce you would expect from restoration comedy.

Playing with biography

One amusing element in the novel is its exposure to how impossible it is to really write autobiography. The narrator of *Orlando* tries to write Orlando's biography, which is difficult because s/he lives for so long and has two genders. But even those whose lives seem more straightforward, it is suggested, can only be represented in biographies as versions of a fictionalised character the biographer has invented for their own ends.

Orlando is a funny and thoughtful feminist novel which uses what Julia Kristeva calls 'women's time' as well as both changing identities and genders.

THE WAVES (1931)

In *The Waves*, her most experimental novel, Virginia Woolf moves further away from the nineteenth century novel. There are five main characters whom we follow through childhood to maturity, but their stories are not told straightforwardly. Each character delivers a voiced interior monologue using their own representative symbols. The style and imagery of the speech of each character varies to express their particular world view, and the style matures as do the outlooks expressed, as the characters mature. The characters who speak are Bernard, Rhoda, Jinny, Susan, Neville and Louis. There is a seventh character whose thoughts we never hear, but of whom it has been suggested all the others are contributory parts. He is the pivotal character, Percival, and he dies in the novel (this invites comparison with Virginia Woolf's brother Thoby). Bernard is the voice heard most often, the phrasemaker, the writer.

As they grow older all the characters are forced to choose ways to live and their personalities become fixed. Bernard recognises that he has a multiple self – he could be many things other than what he has chosen to be:

> I am not one person; I am many people; I do not altogether know who I am – Jinny, Susan, Neville, Rhoda or Louis – or how to distinguish my life from theirs.

We are composed of those we know, our friends help to mould us.

Woolf deals with questions of how the self relates to the world, fits in, becomes defined and limited, understands the world by patterns and structures. Bernard wonders 'How describe the world seen without a self', feels certainties dissolve. He chooses to live and to write, by writing making a mark on the world and on history.

Techniques – choric voices, rhythms

Woolf uses particular phrases and symbols to characterise the different ways in which people see the world. In *The Waves* the ways in which different characters speak, see the world, the images they use to represent reality change each time a different character appears. Each produces an internal monologue representing a different world view, and as they come together, the language and symbolism of one character overlaps with that of another, producing a sense of the two meeting and interacting. This is a form of intersubjectivity. The children grow into adults and each responds as if a chorus. The novel is like a piece of music with different threads or musical themes, the different voices, and a chorus as they come together.

What the young people do forms one part of the novel. As they grow up, so the waves and sun on the beach change their angle and mood.

Each different section which marks a different phase in their lives is begun with a passage looking at nature, the waves on the beach. This captures both the natural mood which reflects their lives, and suggests that life and nature carry on whatever happens to people. The eternal pulse of life, the cyclical pattern of nature which underlies all man's life and structures is suggested by the repeated image of the waves and the seasons, and the sun's movement during a day.

Woolf's most experimental novel, *The Waves* is a poetic exploration of how different friends experience and reflect their versions of reality, evoked not with straightforward character, plot, theme, action, description, but poetically, with interior monologue, rhythms and symbols. Woolf's last two novels, *In Between the Acts* and *The Years* are suggested for further reading.

Contemporary Critical Approaches

THE MOVE AWAY FROM REALISM

Virginia Woolf has a very different style from the realist novelists. Critically, we should not be surprised she was received badly by many realist novelists, especially Arnold Bennett, and very well indeed by the other experimental writers, particularly the literary modernists such as T.S. Eliot and Katherine Mansfield.

A woman, upper class, privileged, and in the centre not only of London, but of literary modernism at the beginning and in the early years of this century, Woolf spearheaded changes, both in style and in the form and expectations we have of the novel, which have influenced radical texts since her day. A contemporary of James Joyce, who wrote *Portrait of the Artist as a Young Man* and *Ulysses*, Woolf shares with him the representation of reality reclaimed and presented as it is felt from the inside. Hers is work which captures the sense of experience as it impinges upon the consciousness, which captures reality as lived by the individual.

Woolf's own comments about the literature she found around her serve as a useful introduction to the innovatory nature of her work. Reading Bennett and Galsworthy, the stolid, heavy, later realists of the end of the nineteenth century, she felt that for all their solidity, they were at the mercy of a very constricting literary version of what reality should be.

David Lodge, in *After Bakhtin*, talks of literary modernism and of Woolf, saying that the modernist novel was characteristically a novel of consciousness, of the subconscious and the unconscious, of memory, reverie, introspection and dream. Woolf, like Joyce, Lawrence and

Faulkner, presents 'the subjectivity of experience and the relativity of truth'.

A useful anthology of works of Woolf criticism is edited by Majumdar and McLaurin (1975) (see Further Reading) which contains the full breadth of work on Woolf, from reviews to obituaries.

Woolf establishes her reputation

E.M. Forster's essay (1926) shows us that the initial response to Virginia Woolf was to see her as a talented impressionistic writer who produced very beautiful, but rather difficult prose. She was part of the group of avant-garde writers including James Joyce, Dorothy Richardson and Katherine Mansfield who wrote 'stream of consciousness' work which many critics felt avoided the representation of external realities and which seemed rather non-historical, as a contrast to the very solid realism from Wells and Bennett. Gradually, her work grew in recognition and stature and very positive critical comments were made by the great writers of the day. T.S. Eliot admired her, as did William Empson and the novelist Storm Jameson. From 1927 onwards, after the publication of *To the Lighthouse*, she established a reputation.

The first book on her work was written by Winifred Holtby, also a novelist. Her *Virginia Woolf: A Critical Memoir* (1932) was very perceptive, particularly about *Jacob's Room*, and her comparisons between the ways in which the narrative runs and the way cinema montage works have been influential in understanding Woolf's work. Her use of images and her colliding of responses, events and feelings can be seen as cinematic in their effect. In contrast, Jean Guiguet's 1965 study, represents her as concerned with existential questions about identity, the self and existence.

Several influences harmed her critical reputation. F.R. Leavis's critical views of her work were important as were the influences of the journal *Scrutiny*. A common complaint from critics during the 1930s was that her works were obscure. Such critics preferred more realistic, historical works that were politically engaged in an overt way. Her techniques were too subtle for many 'common readers'. Some missed the irony and the perception, finding only the experimental writing. Many critics argued that she was not actually writing novels, but prose poetry. The next step was to find within this form the cause of unsatisfactory characterisation and plot. Nor could critics cope with her focus on gendered experience, which did not receive favourable responses until the psychoanalytical/biographical and feminist criticism of the 1970s.

Arnold Bennett criticised her drawing of character and her representing of outward events. Most critics found her first two novels, *The Voyage Out* and *Night and Day* more manageable than the later, more experimental works. But the experimental work was appreciated by the great experimental modernists.

T.S. Eliot wrote of *Jacob's Room* that it:

> compels very careful reading because there is a great deal of excitement in reading it...it seems to me that you have really accomplished what you set out to do in this book, and that you have freed yourself from any compromise between the traditional novel and your original gift.
>
> (letter to Virginia Woolf – 4 Dec 1922)

WOOLF AS INNOVATOR

Arnold Bennett (1923) said that she 'couldn't create characters that survive' and J Middleton Murray (1923) argued that Woolf was one of the new writers who brought the novel 'to an impasse' because of her neglect of plot or story. Woolf herself decided to break new ground and follow her convictions that her way of writing was going to be effective and successful. She comments in her diary 'My theory is that at 40 one either increases the pace or slows down'. (Bell and McNeillie, 1977–84, entry 28 July 1923 vol ii p 259). Like Mrs Dalloway herself, Woolf plunges in, deciding to write about 'the world seen by the sane and the insane, side by side'. (*Ibid* 14 Oct 1922 ii p207).

Her diary reveals much about her intentions with her novels as well as her reactions to critics. Following vast amounts of speculation about the meaning of the lighthouse in *To the Lighthouse*, she suggests that it is an artistic construction and:

> 'I meant *nothing* by the lighthouse. One has to have a central line down the middle of the book to hold the design together.'
>
> (*Ibid* 15 October 1923 ii p270–1)

In 1926, E.M. Forster's essay 'The novels of Virginia Woolf' (Vol XV, no 3 April 1926 p505-514) notes that Woolf has made a 'definite contribution' to the novel by her power to convey 'the actual process of thinking', but he found her characters unsatisfactory. He said they did not 'live'.

Critics commented on her ability to capture family relationships (Quentin Bell, 1971) and to represent an inter-relationship between individuals and the organic work, continued existence, a kind of Romantic perception (Anna Benjamin, 1963), where people and the natural world relate to each other and people do not dominate or control it.

A line of critical appreciation developed as critics started to look closely at the symbolism in her work. Some concentrated on the symbol of the lighthouse in *To the Lighthouse*, but others linked her symbolism to her main concerns. John Lehmann in '*Virginia Woolf: writers of today*' (London Vol 2 ed. Denys Val Baker 1948 p73-84) argues that Woolf 'enlarged the sensibility of her time and changed English literature'. Through her 'memorable' symbols she expressed something unusual, the mystery of life and death and love, its beauties and terrors. But on the other hand, Leavis and his followers (backed by Marxist critics, Bradbrook and Rohr) attacked her for her 'obsession' with purely aesthetic sensibility, saying she had no concern with moral issues.

BETWEEN POETRY AND FICTION

The arguments about Woolf in terms of private and public continued into the later twentieth century and beyond between critics such as Snaith and Bowlby.

Other close textual readings produced celebratory comments on her interior monologue and stream of consciousness. David Daiches's work comments on the interior monologue in *Mrs Dalloway* (*Virginia Woolf: the novel and the modern world*, Chicago 1939 p158-187), arguing that the instabilities of the period led Woolf to abstract and refine life, producing 'something between lyrical poetry and fiction'. Empsons close reading of *To the Lighthouse* (*Virginia Woolf: scrutinies by various writers* London ed E Rickword) praises her sensitiveness but disapproves of her impressionistic method. Irene Simon provides a detailed and sound analysis of her imagery in her major fiction, analysing her structurally ('Some aspects of Virginia Woolf's imagery'; *English Studies*, Amsterdam vol 41 no 3 June 1966 p180–196).

ADMIRATION OVERSEAS

If she met with mixed reactions at home, Woolf was held in high esteem on the continent. Famous French critics such as Andre Maurois and Jacque-Emile Blanche admired her works, praising her psychological insight and lyrical prose and her treatment of sexual relations. Her work excited interest in America, Japan and India – all over the world.

＊＊＊＊*SUMMARY*＊＊＊＊

- Woolf was seen by the literary establishment as too aesthetic and 'literary'.

- She was supported and appreciated by other modernist writers.

- Arguments about her work continued into the late twentieth century and beyond.

---

7 Modern Critical Approaches

MODERN CRITICAL APPROACHES

Between 1941 and the late 1970s there were few studies on Woolf, and then she became very popular again and a wide range of work followed. Her work since this time has been viewed from a myriad of angles, ranging from technique to feminism to the autobiographical and even the realist readings. The most popular critique of Woolf included those which take either a feminist angle, seeing her as a proto feminist, or those which look at her work from a biographical and psychoanalytic standpoint. Among the main critics we might include Jacqueline Rose, Roger Pole, Stephen Trombley, Mark Hussey, Jane Marcus and Michelle Barrett. More recently, younger critics such as Anna Snaith have joined the critical arena and there is a now yearly conference entirely devoted to Woolf's work which focuses on a full set of approaches and themes. It seems she can be read using any critical approaches at all.

PSYCHOANALYTIC APPROACHES

Psychoanalytic approaches concentrate on such issues as:

* Treatment of self, subjectivity and consciousness within texts.

* The analysis of the effect and treatment of dreams, nightmares, imagination.

* Symbolism as it reveals imagination at work and hidden/covert meaning and tendencies.

* The psychology of characters within the text.

* The psychology of the author as it reveals itself through their treatment of various issues and use of imagery, e.g. pathology and the macabre.

* The psychology of an age which causes/conditions the production of certain sorts of text and interest.

* The hidden motives and needs of character, of situation, of story development as revealed through imagery and through action which can be read to illustrate the working of the mind e.g. repetitive actions, actions hiding feelings/revealing feelings.

* Imagery and symbolism.

Psychoanalytical criticism also incorporates biographical material. It starts to make links between the life of the author and events of characters in their works, focusing on the representation of the self and relationships with others and the significances and resonances of places and events.

AUTOBIOGRAPHY AND PSYCHOANALYSIS

A popular critical approach which has embraced Woolf is that which delves into a mixture of autobiography and psychoanalysis, investigating what it is in her life and her work which explores states of consciousness, versions of self and of the world. This looks at details of her upbringing, her relationship with her parents and family and with her half brothers George and Gerald, and also at her moments of mental disturbance. It recognises this 'madness' as both an alternative, if suppressed, mode of vision and as a series of disturbances which shattered her calm and left her depressed. Some critics trace elements of her life in her works. Others explore the states of consciousness she is able to represent through streams of consciousness and other modes. They celebrate the ways in which she can explore the self, changing relationships and changing experiences and representation of felt reality.

Experience into fiction

Early drafts and diary entries show Woolf translating her own experiences into her fictions (see comments on *To the Lighthouse* above). Of course, many writers and particularly women writers have been subjected to the intrusions of autobiographical reading of their work, the extreme case of which leads to a substitution of our reading the life rather than the works. But in Woolf's case, a well-handled biographical and psychoanalytic approach yields much that is of interest in relation to the ways she manages her own search for identity as a woman and writer. It also explores how she sees her position in relation to her parents, brother and sister, as well as her friends and her lovers. Some of the chief elements of her life which tend to be explored in this approach include her relationship with her parents, the intellectual Leslie Stephen and her nurturing mother Julia. Also important is her abuse at the hands of her half brother George (more recently explored by critics including Poole and Trombley,) which seems to surface in some of the less pleasant sexual encounters such as that of Rachel Vinrace with Richard Dalloway in *The Voyage Out*. Her relationship with Vita Sackville West also figures, amusingly and ironically informing the representation of the adventure of the androgynous Orlando, in *Orlando* and in Sally Seton in *Mrs Dalloway*. Some of the elements of her own breakdowns appear in Septimus Warren Smith's breakdown, and the dissolution of Rhoda in *The Waves*.

Diaries and papers

In 1953 Leonard Woolf published *A Writer's Diary*, a one volume selection of passages from the 30 manuscripts of her diary. In 1972 her nephew Quentin Bell published a two volume biography followed by edited diaries and letters. Her *Diary* edited by Anne Olivier Bell and Andrew McNeillie was published in five volumes between 1977 and 1984, as well as six volumes of her letters. After Leonard's death in 1969 his own and Virginia's papers, deposited with the University of Sussex library, were made available, and since then both different sketches and versions of her novels have appeared.

Bell and Marcus

Jane Marcus' work, written from a socialist feminist point of view, insists on the existence of a political element in her work ('Tintinnabulations storming the toolshed'; and 'Quentin's bogey' in *Art and Anger* 1988). She argues that Quentin Bell's work on Woolf is marred by his disapproval of her life as a woman, and his playing down her lifetime of political engagement. Bell sees Woolf as a 'frigid snob, invalid lady or mad witch'. Her own version is quite different – her self description as a great goddess. Recent biographies such as Lyndal Gordon's *Virginia Woolf: a Writer's Life* focus on how Woolf recreated herself as a writer. She sees Woolf as a visionary and plays down the information about abuse and suffering.

Poole and Trombley

Roger Poole's work, *The Unknown Virginia Woolf* (1980) challenges representations of her as mad and perceives Leonard Woolf as an insensitive, excessively rational, dominant man who exercised power over Virginia, insisting that she be regulated and put under the control of doctors whenever her hard work drove her to breakdown. His reading of her diary and suicide notes explores and explains links between the troubled self and the writing, and relates her inner life, such as we can explore it, with her fictions. It is very much in line with the kinds of reading of madness put forward by such writers as R.D. Laing, which see it as socially constructed. This view appears also in feminist criticism and is both liberating and potentially rather suspect too (not all bouts of breakdown are breakthroughs). Stephen Trombley's *All that summer she was mad* (1980) examines the work of the doctors who treated Woolf, for information about their opinion of what madness is in relation to her. He argues that those who called her mad were themselves imposing a reading on her reactions, these men were indeed monstrous in their treatment of her (see them explored in the figure of Sir William Bradshaw in *Mrs Dalloway*).

An early work, Jean Guiguet's *Virginia Woolf And Her Works* (first published in French in 1962) sees her through Sartrean **existentialist** perspectives as trying to find a sense of identity and self.

KEYWORD

Existentialism Jean-Paul Sartre developed a philosophy termed 'existentialism' according to which we experience a sense of 'being' in the world which is immediate and exists before labels and words. There are no absolute values or beliefs: we invest in a system of beliefs because it is good in itself.

Richter and Hussey

Harvena Richter's *Virginia Woolf: the Inward Voyage* sees Woolf throughout her work as both recognising and denying 'the abyss', that is the meaninglessness of life and her loss of self identity. Richter looks at Woolf's work as being concerned with modes of perception and the multiplicity of self – and the focus of her novels on moments such as when a character reflects on who s/he could be, or feels some sense of strangeness or loss of reality, reflects perception about self and existence. Mark Hussey's *The Singing of the Real World: the philosophy of VirginiaWoolf's fiction* organises characters by theme and refuses to impose on Woolf a single contiguous philosophical argument. Instead he reflects and discusses her variety, her anxieties and the ways in which she explores her various thoughts and arguments through her own language. This refusal of a single reading is in line with similar refusals in recent feminist critics such as Bowlby and Snaith. Hussey sees Woolf as fascinated by a world apprehended by the central core of self, rather than the 'apparition' or the roles we play in public. She is searching, in her use of stream of consciousness, for the pre-verbal expression, what we feel and sense, before putting it into words.

Recently psychobiographical studies such as that by Louise de Salvo (1989) point out the sexual threat permeating the household that Woolf grew up in, but it questions the advisability of seeing as fixed truths events we can only guess about. The links between life and her explorations of experience and perception in her works, are all aided by psychobiography but there are dangers of reading too much into the link, and it is a particular danger women writers seem more exposed to than men.

FEMINIST CRITICAL APPROACHES

Feminist criticism

Feminist critical practices and strategies involve:

* The study of women as represented in male written texts, in female written texts, in time and in context.

* Studying how culture and social forms affect gender as represented in all texts.

* The investigation, definition and analysis of a specifically female mode of writing.

* Analysing women's writing and the process of publishing as they are related to gender. Considering the woman reader and her response to texts.

* Examining a broader base than the term feminist implies. This focuses us on the cultural production of texts in context, and the inscription of gender roles by writers, and of writers, within texts.

Feminist approaches to Woolf

Contemporary feminist critics on Woolf see her as a proto or early feminist, a tremendously influential mother of the novel. The comments she has made about the roles of women, the representations of what is or is not available to women, even the representations of different male and female minds is highly original and has been unsurpassed in all the years since. One of her contemporary inheritors is Jeannette Winterson who identifies with Woolf and her achievements.

> We think back through our mothers if we are women. It is useless to go to the great men writers for help, however much one may go to them for pleasure.
>
> ('A Room of One's Own' pp.72–3).

Literary foremother

A good summary of the variety of approaches to Woolf's work can be found in Mary Eagleton's *Feminist Criticism*. Several feminist critics embrace Woolf's work as pivotal in their own, or question why some other critics find it so unacceptable to link life and works. Louis de Salvo and Sara Ruddick (1984) write confessionally about how Woolf's novels have inspired them to find their own voices. Carolyn Heilbrun in *Writing a Woman's life* connects identity and literary problems using Woolf as a prime example. Since the 1970s women critics have used

Woolf's work as that of a literary foremother; one whose challenges to patriarchal values and ways of seeing and expressing the world and the self set a model for other women's challenges, in literature and in life. Elaine Showalter began some of this work although she wrote negatively of Woolf as a feminist (1978 – *A Literature Of Their Own*). Critics carried on with a focus on Woolf through the writing of Jane Marcus, especially in 'Virginia Woolf: a feminist slant' (1983) and subsequent essays. This recognises a literary challenge and start to the way we see the world as it appears particularly in Woolf's poetical essays, 'A Room of One's Own' and 'Three Guineas' and as it is acted out in her novels. Jane Marcus has gone on to look at Woolf and postcolonialism.

FEMINIST PSYCHOANALYTICAL READINGS

A number of feminist critics have furthered Woolf's exploration of states of consciousness and of the self. In 1973 Nancy Topping Bazin developed a psychoanalytical reading of Woolf's interrelations to the argument on androgyny which Woolf herself explored in her essays and dramatised in *Orlando*. Bazin sees Woolf working out a manic depressive routine as she moves through her mother's influence (the manic) and her father's (the depressive). This very psychoanalytic reading is related to others such as that of Roger Poole, but also marks a phase of feminist psychoanalytic reading in the 1970s.

Arguments rage within feminist criticism about Woolf's representations of and response to issues such as real time, real place, real politics, real events, and her flight from reality, her exploration of consciousness and subjective states of being. Patrica Stubbs' *Women and Fiction* (1979) argues that Woolf 'actually devitalised her fictional world' by her focus on subjectivity and her aesthetic theories. On the other hand, Michelle Barrett (1979) argues quite the opposite, that Woolf's strength lies in her ability to recognise and explore women's lives in their historical contexts of the material experience, although she certainly would enable these to be expressed through personal responses, or fictionalised scenarios. Critics have difficulties with Woolf's arguments about the necessary androgyny of a writer.

Phyllis Rose's *Woman of Letters* (1978) recognises feminism as the central pivot of Woolf's life and sees her works as explorations of gendered problems of identity and lifehood. Unlike Roger Poole, she views Woolf's marriage as achieving a supportive intimacy rather than an oppositional relationship.

Bowlby

More recently Rachel Bowlby's *Feminist Destinations* (1988) uses the analogy of railway or linear travel to investigate the kind of feminist journeys Woolf takes in her works. Bowlby rightly asserts that Woolf is the only woman writer 'to be taken seriously by critics of all casts' whether they like her work or not. She argues how in both Woolf's essays – notably 'Mr Bennett and Mrs Brown' which takes place on a railway journey – and in her novels, Woolf traces the differences between the potentially highly rigid linearity of a masculine mind and the varied, multiple perspective and multiple interpretations open to a feminist writer and a woman's perception. Bowlby illustrates how Woolf can deal with material and economic, historic conditions which affect men's and women's lives, and their ways of viewing the world, their perceptions and imaginative responses. In *To the Lighthouse* Mr Ramsay's world view is logical and linear but it is limiting, rigid, despairing. The step from one logical step to the next is compared to letters of the alphabet and contrasts with women's outsider position. But women are also seen as offering a different kind of tour through life, through thought patterns, which are more flexible and fluid, various and able to hold oppositions in harmony. This emerges in decisions made in *Mrs Dalloway*. Bowlby examines Woolf's statement of structures of sexual difference and aligns these with her understanding of biographical and historical narratives. For example, in *Orlando* the playfulness with both history and biography challenge conventional representations of these two forms. Another example of this can be found in *In Between the Acts* where language is shown to be unstable in constructing collective fictions of history and identity.

Snaith

Anna Snaith's *Virginia Woolf: Public and Private Negotiations* (2000) sees in Woolf's life and works a unity between terms often represented as dichotomous-public and private. She argues that there is a political agenda behind this representation: 'a public and private dichotomy then is integral to women's history in that it has worked as a conceptual justification for various practices of patriarchal oppression' (p9). She concentrates on how Woolf refuses this dichotomy and renegotiates spaces and places. Woolf shows how the prioritisation of the domestic space has repressed women and prevented them from taking part in everyday activities of the world – commerce, travel, work, education. Woolf, Snaith argues, shifts the use of the term 'separate spheres' for men and women; her women trespass onto lawns and into libraries, ('A Room of One's Own') or they travel across London (*Mrs Dalloway*). Their roles as outsiders ('Three Guineas') is highlighted and questioned. Woolf herself was active in both public and private spaces, and even Leonard Woolf acknowledges these different phases in her life and work saying she was 'the least political animal' but also 'the last person who could ignore the political menaces under which we all lived'. Woolf is very engaged with the political menace of war in particular. She also enabled a focus on the historical and material as well as private subjectivity. Public and private was a dichotomy of the period which Woolf challenged in her life and work as she did others (e.g. between men and women) 'her feminism and pacifism in the 1930s were founded on the *continuity* between public and private realms, the oppression found in the public realm being linked to that of the private.' (Snaith, p 13)

A useful collection of critical essays is *Virginia Woolf* by Julia Briggs (1994), while a book which helps link the life and the works is Hermione Lee's *Virginia Woolf* (1996) which unites a feminist exploration of her works with a detailed scrutiny of her life. Through this rich book we can read and feel how and when Virginia made different decisions, how she responded to events which she transmuted into fictions, how she reacted to reviewers, how she lived her life.

✳✳✳✳SUMMARY✳✳✳✳

- A popular approach to Woolf has been a synthesis of biographical and psychoanalytical perspectives.

- This mix provides much that is of interest both about Woolf and her work.

- There are many different and often contradictory feminist readings of Woolf.

---

8 Where Next?

Reading more books by Virginia Woolf is an obvious first step! And as well as reading novels by Woolf, try her short stories and her essays, many of which are very amusing and all of which are very well written and insightful. Look in the Chronology (page 77) for an indication of when each work was published.

THE VOYAGE OUT (1915)

The Voyage Out gives us an insightful picture of everyday life of late Victorian/early twentieth century upper middle class young women, rather like Woolf herself. Indeed, it is partly a fictionalised version of Woolf's life. The novel starts and finishes 'in media res' – in the middle of actions, without detailed information on history and background appearing first, and without neat endings. It is also a mixture of a storyline, i.e. events which happen to Rachel, and a poetic piece about inner feelings, symbolic moods. Rachel Vinrace is a young woman, the central character, who travels in her father's ship to South America. The novel is essentially about her travelling, growing up, finding out about love and her own sexuality, and dying after contracting a fever following a boat trip on a jungle river. The novel is also concerned with women's lives in particular. It shows a young girl's development into maturity and untimely death just as she seems to have found love.

The novel is not as experimental as Woolf's later works, and therefore more accessible to most readers. It has fairly conventionally created characters and a plot and is concerned with asking questions about what is of value in life, and other social and philosophical questions.

NIGHT AND DAY (1919)

Night and Day has been seen as Woolf's traditional nineteenth century realistic novel (before she wrote more experimentally). She creates solid characters and places them in realised settings with credible dialogue and a plot with a beginning, middle and end. Here we find Woolf concentrating on the everyday existence of women and on the destructiveness of attitudes that led to and through the Great War. Her statement: 'Let us not take it for granted that life exists in what is more commonly thought big than in what is commonly thought small' (1919) emphasises her reactions against the war (which avoids the everyday social life) and her celebration of the lives of women as well as a statement of her beliefs and practices as a modernist.

Night and Day is interesting from the point of view of its treatment of the position of women. Mary Datchet is the unpaid secretary working for a suffragette society and Woolf shows her own feelings, that long term service in the suffrage movement is not the way to gain gender equality, and in fact removes those people who take part in such labours from the normal run of life.

It is a novel of social manners. Woolf's characters, rather like those of Jane Austen in such novels as *Pride and Prejudice* or *Emma*, first fall in love with the wrong person, before finding their match. The novel deals with social interactions and constraints that surround the characters' development. It is amusing, and as such is both like and unlike her later work, for Woolf's ironies and amusing awareness of social blunders and gaffes as well as delicate difficult nuances of behaviour have often been overlooked by critics. It is also a dark novel in many ways. The criticism of women's constrained lives and of the dangerous lies of romantic fiction (leading to domestic limitations on women and men) predominate in the presentation of final settled relationships meaning that all will not always be well.

JACOB'S ROOM (1922)

Jacob's Room really bears witness to the start of Woolf's experiments with new techniques, particularly her challenges to conventions of the novel, and her first use of stream of consciousness. It is also a direct indictment of the cruel waste of young life of the First World War. It is both a historically contextualised novel and one which uses poetic prose, challenging the characteristics of realism. It is more straightforward to read than many of the later works.

The novel is closely aligned with the political arguments of Woolf's more polemical, long essay 'Three Guineas'. This makes direct connections between the insistence upon logic, order, boundaries, divisiveness, differences, hierarchies, and the destructiveness of imperialistic war that kills young men. Technically, it is innovative. There is little story or plot and all conventional transitions from character to character and from place to place have been abolished as Woolf works by impressions.

Woolf sets out to prove the points she made in her essay 'Modern Fiction', for here the accent doesn't fall on the most obvious elements. In fact what would seem elsewhere to be the most important incidents are referred to casually. Jacob's death is one such example. It isn't referred to except in the discussion about what to do with his boots, which are all that remain of him apart from memories, after he is killed in the war.

IN BETWEEN THE ACTS (1941)

This novel concentrates on a group of friends and acquaintances, and how they see the world. It also deals with structures, versions of time and reality. There is to be a pageant at Pointz Hall and the actors are grouped and presented by a woman with boundless creative energy, Miss La Trobe. Like Lily Briscoe, and Virginia Woolf herself, she is a creative artist and desires order and harmony, and to present her view of things to her audience. Only fragments of the speeches are wafted to the audience. One aspect of this novel that is memorable, is the evocation of prehistoric times, the suggestion that the prehistoric past is living on today, that history is part of life. It is a dramatic attempt to evoke the sense of historic time.

THE YEARS (1937)

Woolf's last work, *The Years*, is a period novel. Fifty-seven years are divided into arbitrary time divisions. This novel has been seen by some as rather a regression because it is not as experimental in format as *The Waves* for example. However, it became a bestseller in the United States. A chronicle of a family through three generations, it suggests corresponding changes in the social, political and cultural atmosphere. *The Years* started life as *The Pargiters*, but the novel and the polemical essay within this earlier text were then separated into two. It is based on the classic text *Antigone*, a tale in which the sister, Antigone, pleads for the burial of her dead brother. *The Years* is an elegy on lost brothers. It celebrates sibling love as an alternative to marriage which it indicts as a primeval swamp which drowns men and women.

OTHER MODERNISTS

There are other writers it would also be useful to read. The writers of the Bloomsbury group are a good start, including T.S. Eliot, *Collected poems*, *The Waste land*, *The Four Quartets*, Katherine Mansfield, *At the Bay, Prelude, The Garden Party*, E.M. Forster *Passage to India, Howards End, Room with a View, Where Angels fear to Tread*, poetry by H.D. (Hilda Doolittle), *Collected poems*, Edith Sitwell, *Collected poems*, prose by Dorothy Richardson *Pilgrimage*, and other women writers of the period who also ask questions about women's roles and lives, such as Kate Chopin *The Awakening*, Charlotte Perkins Gilman, *The Yellow Wallpaper*. You will find that several of these writers, like Woolf, are seeking for something to believe in, and for a sense of identity in the changing and demanding world of the early part of the twentieth century. They are also quite experimental, playing with words, refusing the formulae and conventions of the nineteenth-century novel and some of the rather dull repetitive poetry of the nineteenth century.

Look at some other twentieth-century writers who have developed the ideas of stream of consciousness and interior monologue.

✳ Read or go and see Beckett *Waiting for Godot* or *Malone Dies*.

* Doris Lessing takes on many of the thoughts Woolf begins, about war, women, imagination, and her *The Golden Notebook, The Summer Before the Dark, Briefing for a Descent into Hell* are all powerful novels to read. They concentrate on versions of madness or breakdown, also, and see it as a breakthrough.

* Read Angela Carter *The Magic Toyshop, Nights at the Circus* and Jeanette Winterson (who says she inherits Woolf's style and interests) *Oranges are not the Only fruit, Sexing the Cherry*. These contemporary women writers also investigate women's and men's roles, and use language most creatively and beautifully, as does Woolf.

The Woolf annual comes out yearly from Mark Hussey at PACE in the USA. There is a yearly conference, and there is a Woolf society which meets, reads, discusses, visits her homes in Bloomsbury and Richmond. You too can visit her homes and the places where the Bloomsbury group used to meet. In Gordon Square and Taviton Street in central London near the University, a short walk from Euston station (and a stone's throw from Dickens' house in Doughty Street) are blue plaques commemorating Woolf and other Bloomsbury group members. Visit Sissinghurst in Kent where Vita Sackville West used to live, and enjoy the beautiful gardens and old buildings.

Woolf is a serious writer who is ironic, astute, perceptive and very enjoyable. We hope you continue to enjoy her work.

Glossary

Existentialism Jean-Paul Sartre developed a philosophy termed 'existentialism', according to which we experience a sense of 'being' in the world which is immediate and exists before labels and words. There are no absolute values or beliefs: we invest in a system of beliefs because it is good in itself.

Free indirect speech This captures someone's words without actually quoting what they say – it projects us into their mind.

Freud Psychoanalyst Sigmund Freud is credited with arguing that we develop identity as we grow from childhood, much adult feeling and behaviour derives from early childhood sexual experience, dreams are a key to our unconscious and our unconscious is when we repress fears, sexual fantasies and threats. Discovering the unconscious helps us understand self and others, and to treat psychotic or troubled behaviours (via analysis).

Inner time or 'durée' Bergson: Henri Bergson was a French writer and philosopher in the latter part of the nineteenth century. Like Bergson, Woolf felt that time, our inner sense of time passing, needed to be expressed other than in a rigidly chronological fashion with events and changes marked discreetly. Events close together she felt must influence the present, the present the future, the future the present, the past the future – and additionally, we all experience a sense of the flow of time differently in different contexts.

Interior monologue The voice speaking to you about what you are doing inside your head. It is a flow of thoughts expressed as words, with sentences usually starting 'I...' and is a kind of commentary on how someone is feeling and what they are experiencing.

Intersubjectivity How different people's responses affect each other. Woolf concentrates on a group of friends or family and shows how their feelings about each other affect their attitudes and actions, and are also influenced by thoughts of the past and the future.

Jung Psychoanalyst and great thinker, Jung developed a theory that we categorise people as archetypes. He used images and metaphors to describe how people develop a sense of identity, relate to others and behave.

Modernism A term used to describe the literary movement of the 1890s–1940s whose international writers numbered among them T.S. Eliot, Virginia Woolf, James Joyce and Ezra Pound. They wanted to write in a new way, rejecting the tired conventions of the nineteenth century and wished to 'make it new'. Complex technically, they often concentrated on disillusionment, fragmentation, and a search for something to believe in.

Patriarchy An oppressive system of control which is dominated by male power. The word derives

from 'patriarch', father, head of the family, but is used not to suggest men as such but an oppressive system which subordinates women and is probably highly nationalistic.

Post Impressionism Artistic movement in which the whole is made up of many different elements in different colours, and seen from a distance it forms a certain shape, a different picture to that seen up close.

Psychoanalysis Analysis based on the self, the psyche, it was established early in the twentieth century and spearheaded by Jung and Freud.

Performativity – roles and constructions In the latter part of the twentieth century, theorists have written a great deal about the construction of versions of self in a shared world. Judith Butler, for instance, argues that we are all performers, we put on versions of self, roles, we are constructs, our sense of identity and our behaviour are constructed and these constructs we adopt. Everything is constructed. This awareness of role play, artifice, constructedness, of gender roles in particular, does not need to lead to a real sense of dissolution, disorder, but an awareness which can lead to parody, handling the act. Woolf's representations and explorations predate these mid-twentieth and late-twentieth-century explorations.

Realist novel A term particularly associated with the nineteenth-century novel to refer to the idea that texts appear to represent the world as it really is.

Semi-fictionalised autobiography Writing about oneself which has fictionalised or elaborated/imagined elements. A form used by the African American writer Maya Angelou.

Solipsism Being wrapped up in oneself, a kind of separateness of the individual self from the self enacted as a set of roles in the shared social world. The psychoanalyst R.D. Laing also wrote about solipsism, and about breakdown as being a kind of potential breakthrough, and the American novelist Ken Kesey's *One Flew Over the Cuckoo's Nest*

questioned definitions of conformity and sanity. Solipsism relates the notion of feeling separate as a self from the social world, questioning what seems to be commonly accepted as reality, as a position which was not only radical but imaginative, creative and positive.

Stream of consciousness A new way of representing reality and experience as we feel it; the thoughts, feelings and sensations of an individual, all flowing together.

Suffragettes The suffragettes, led by Christabel and Emmeline Pankhurst, were a number of women who campaigned actively for gender equality and specifically the vote or suffrage. One suffragette threw herself in front of the king's horse at the Derby, others chained themselves to railings and were imprisoned and force fed. After the First World War, women gained the vote (if over 30 and a householder).

CHRONOLOGY OF MAJOR WORKS

1904   Publishes her first review in the *Guardian*.

1905   Beginning of the Bloomsbury group. Virginia lectures at Morley College, an institute for working men and women.

1907   Begins work on first novel, *Melymbrosia*, later published as *The Voyage Out*.

1913   Completes *The Voyage Out*.

1917   Virginia and Leonard Woolf found the Hogarth Press.

1918   Woolf begins work on her second novel, *Night and Day*.

1919   *Night and Day* published by Gerald Duckworth.

1922   *Jacob's Room* is published by Hogarth Press. After this Woolf publishes all her own novels in England. (James Joyce's *Ulysses* and T.S. Eliots's *The Waste Land* published.)

1925   Publishes *Mrs Dalloway* and the collection of essays 'The Common Reader'.

1927   Publishes *To the Lighthouse*, plans *The Jessemy Brides* (*Orlando*.)

1928   Publishes *Orlando*, dedicated to Vita Sackville-West. Woolf delivers lectures at the two Cambridge women's colleges, Newnham and Girton. These lectures later develop into 'A Room of One's Own'.

1929   Publishes 'A Room of One's Own' and the essay 'Women and Fiction'. Begins work on a novel *The Moths*, later *The Waves*.

1931   Publishes *The Waves*.

1932   Publishes a second collection of essays, 'The Second Common Reader'.

1933   Publishes *Flush*, a novel about the relationship between Elizabeth Browning and Robert Browning, from the point of view of Elizabeth's dog, Flush.

1937   Publishes *The Years*, Woolf's first best-seller.

1938   Publishes 'Three Guineas'.

1941   Her novel *Between the Acts* is published posthumously.

Further Reading

Bell, Quentin, *Bloomsbury*, London: Weidenfeld and Nicolson, 1968

Bell, Quentin, *Virginia Woolf: a Biography*, 2 vols, London: Hogarth Press, 1972

Bowlby, Rachel, *Virginia Woolf: Feminist Dimensions*, London: Virago, 1988

Daiches, David, *Virginia Woolf*, (2 edn), Norfolk, Conn, New Directions, 1963

Eagleton, Mary (ed.), *Feminist Literary Criticism*, London: Longman Higher Educational Paperback, 1991

Eagleton, Mary (ed.), *Feminist Literary Theory*, London: Blackwells, 1995

Eagleton, Mary, *Working with Feminist Criticism*, London: Blackwells, 1996

Gordon, Lyndall, *Virginia Woolf: A Writers Life*, Oxford: Oxford University Press, 1984

Guiguet, Jean, *Virginia Woolf and her Works* (trans. Jean Stewart), London, Hogarth Press, 1965

Helibrun, Carolyn, *Writing a Woman's Life*, The Women's Press, 1997

Hussey, Mark, *The Singing of the real World: the philosophy of Virginia Woolf's fiction*, Ohio, Ohio State University Press, 1986

Lee, Hermione, *The Novels of Virginia Woolf*, London: Methuen, 1977

Lee, Hermione, *Virginia Woolf*, London, Chatto & Windus, 1996

Lehman, John, *Virginia Woolf and Her World*, London, Thames & Hudson, 1975

Majumdar, Roger and McLaurin Allen (eds), *Virginia Woolf: The Critical Heritage*, London: Routledge & Keegan Paul, 1975

Marcus, Jane, *New Feminist Essays on Virginia Woolf*, Lincoln, University of Nebraska Press, 1981

Olivier Bell, Anne and McNeillie, *The Diary of Virginia Woolf*, London: Hogarth Press, 5 vol., 1977-1984

Patmore, Coventry, *The Angel in the House*, Haggerston Press, 1998

Poole, Roger, *The Unknown Virginia Woolf*, London, Routledge, 1980

Rose, Phyllis, *Woman of Letters: A Life of Virginia Woolf*, New York: Oxford University Press, 1978

de Salvo, Louise, *Virginia Woolf: the Impact of Childhood Sexual Abuse on her Life and Work*, The Women's Press, 1991

Showalter, Elaine, *A Literature of Their Own*, Virago Press, 1999

Snaith, Anna *Virginia Woolf: Public and Private Negotiations*, Basingstoke, Macmillan, 2000

Trombley, Stephen, *All that Summer she was Mad*, London, Junction Books, 1981

Some internet sites

Virginia Woolf society – also the bulletin, and various research and discussion outlets
http://www.orlando.jp.org/VWSGB/index.html

Virginia Woolf international society
http://cita.scar.utoronto.ca/VWS/Index.html

Index

MARCEL PROUST – A BEGINNER'S GUIDE

Ingrid Wassenaar

Marcel Proust – A Beginner's Guide introduces you to the life and works of Proust. He is shown as a writer who has influenced not only the way we approach literature but also the way we think about ourselves. Discover how *A La Recherche du Temps Perdu* is relevant to today's technology-intensive and individualistic society.

Ingrid Wassenaar's text explores:

- how to approach *A La Recherche du Temps Perdu* (*In Search of Lost Time*)
- Proust's ideas on topics such as time, memory and sexuality
- modern critical approches to Proust and his ideas
- the relevance of these ideas to readers in the twenty-first century.

The facts … the concepts … the ideas …

JAMES JOYCE –
A BEGINNER'S GUIDE

Frank Startup

James Joyce – A Beginner's Guide introduces you to the life and works of one of the most unique and powerful minds of the twentieth century. Focusing on three major works *Dubliners*, *A Portrait of the Artist as a Young Man* and *Ulysses* he explores the background, themes, images and techniques that unite them.

Frank Startup's lively text offers a guide to:

■ plot, setting and character
■ approaching the works
■ how Joyce's works were viewed then and now
■ why you should read Joyce.

The facts … the concepts … the ideas …

CHARLES DICKENS – A BEGINNER'S GUIDE

Rob Abbott and Charlie Bell

Charles Dickens – A Beginner's Guide introduces you to the life and works of Charles Dickens. The book shows him to have been a writer who is both enjoyable and accessible to the modern reader. A great Victorian and prolific novelist Dickens has a profound influence on the way his contemporaries saw their society and the way we today view the Victorians. In exploring four of the most popular novels *Bleak House*, *Oliver Twist*, *Hard Times* and *Great Expectations* the writers show the relevance of Dickens today and help readers to develop their own responses to the works.

Rob Abbott and Charlie Bell's informative text explores:

- how to approach the novels and short stories
- Dickens' ideas on subjects such as morality, poverty and the place of women
- contemporary critical approaches to Dickens and his work
- the influence of Dickens both in his own lifetime and in the twenty-first century.

The facts … the concepts … the ideas …

DOSTOYEVSKY – A BEGINNER'S GUIDE

Rose Miller

Dostoyevsky – A Beginner's Guide introduces you to the life and works of Dostoyevsky. Explore the range and versatility of this thought-provoking and compelling writer, focusing on his concern with writing as a means of understanding the human condition.

Rose Miller's lively text offers:

- an insight into the relationship between the writer's life and his work
- an exploration of characteristic features and recurrent themes in his writing
- an analysis of *Crime and Punishment, The Idiot* and *The Brothers Karamazov*
- an outline of some helpful critical approaches to his style.

The facts … the concepts … the ideas …

SALMAN RUSHDIE – A BEGINNER'S GUIDE

Andrew Blake

Salman Rushdie – A Beginner's Guide introduces you to the life and work of one of the most enjoyable yet controversial contemporary authors. Examining the novels and other writings discover how Rushdie's brilliant prose, and his easy use of popular culture, have helped to inaugurate a new way of writing which expresses the experience of being Indian-English helping us to understand life in the contemporary multicultural world.

Andrew Blake's lively text investigates:

- Rushdie's life and influences
- the novels, short stories and other writings
- Rushdie's recurring use of sources from history, literature and popular culture
- the critical responses to Rushdie's work
- the *Satanic Verses* controversy
- Rushdie's influence on younger writers.

The facts … the concepts … the ideas …

SYLVIA PLATH – A BEGINNER'S GUIDE

Gina Wisker

Sylvia Plath – A Beginner's Guide introduces you to the life and works of one of the most unique and powerful minds of the twentieth century. Focusing on *Daddy, The Bell Jar* and her diaries the writer explores the background, themes, images and techniques that unite them.

Gina Wisker's lively text offers a guide to:

- plot, setting and character
- approaching the works
- how Plath's works were viewed then and now
- why you should read Plath.

The facts … the concepts … the ideas …

SAMUEL BECKETT –
A BEGINNER'S GUIDE

Steve Coots

Samuel Beckett – A Beginner's Guide introduces you to the life and work of one of the great literary figures of the twentieth century, whose work is generally thought to be dark and inaccessible. This highly entertaining book introduces you to Beckett and his work in a clear and illuminating way.

Steve Coots's lively text investigates:

- how to approach the work of Beckett
- Beckett's preoccupations with human existence and the absurdity of the human condition
- the roots of Beckett's vision not just in literature and theatre, but in art, music and comedy.

The facts … the concepts … the ideas …